Crosshill Friday Fellowship .

Helen McCulloch

December 2000

Images

through the

Mists of Time

1939~1945

Helen McLullich

Acknowledgements

Helen McLullich wishes to thank the following for permission to use extracts from copyright works:

BBC: Wartime Announcements; Donald Fisher: Picture and text from *Memories of an Aberfeldy Childhood* by James Fisher, 1989; Perth and Kinross Council: Extract from *Aberfeldy Past and Present* (Dr N.D. Mackay, 1954); Met. Office Edinburgh: Weather forecasts; Reader's Digest Association Ltd: Extracts from *How Britain's Wealth Went West* and *I was Monty's Double*, in *Secrets and Stories from the War* (Vol. 1) © 1963, also an extract from *The Highroad of the Future* from *The Best of 21 Years* © 1960; M.O.D. on behalf of the Controller of HMSO: Reproduction of RAF photos – Sumburgh; Trustees of the Imperial War Museum: for print of Charles Cundall's painting of the Dunkirk Evacuation, and permission to reproduce.

Also the following:

Mitchell Library, Glasgow: for access to Camlachie School's log book; Elizabeth Miskimmin, rector, Breadalbane Academy, Aberfeldy: for access to the school's log book; National Library, Edinburgh: copyright information; Margaret Windgate, headteacher, Garrowhill Primary School: for school photograph and information on school project.

Thanks are also due to Liz Ballantyne, Sheena Bedborough, Ex-provost Hamish Fisher (Aberfeldy) and Gordon Jarvie for their help in the preparation of this book.

Last, but by no means least, my thanks to Raymond MacFadyen for cover design, illustrations, maps, technological assistance and advice ~ and unlimited patience!

Every effort has been made to obtain the necessary permission for material reproduced. Apologies are tendered to any copyright holders who could not be traced.

All profits from the sale of this book to be donated to:

Parkinson's Disease Society
Scottish Resources, 10 Claremont Terrace, Glasgow G3 7XR
Telephone 0141 943 1760

Struan Publishing, 20 Rosefield Gardens,
Uddingston, South Lanarkshire G71 7AW

© Struan Publishing 1999

ISBN 0 9535037 0 4

Typeset in 11pt Palatino
Designed by Cauldron Design Ltd, Berwickshire, Scotland
Printed in Italy by Poligrafico Dehoniana

Foreword

The children I taught in Camlachie School, Gallowgate, Glasgow, in my first year as a teacher. Within two years many of them were war evacuees, some of whom can be readily identified in later pictures in this book. We had a close relationship and I remember these pupils, and other evacuees who joined us in our wartime school, with a deep and lasting affection.

Contents

In memory of my husband,
Ian, who died in April 1997.

CHAPTER 1

Count Down

The rich tapestry of life, unique to each person, has many images woven on its canvas. These will be selectively viewed and reviewed from time to time, conjured up at will or unexpectedly triggered, sometimes by music, but the quality of the images will vary from person to person. Many people will find them strong, detailed and in colours true to their origin: others will find them weak and tantalisingly ephemeral. For a minority, however, no images of the past ~ nor indeed projections into the future ~ will 'flash upon that inward eye'.

The period of my life between the years 1939 and 1945 has been accessed through both visual and auditory imagery more frequently than any other, significantly because 'it was the best of times, it was the worst of times'.

A greyish cloud of uncertainty had hovered over the western world when, in March 1938, Adolf Hitler's Nazi armies took possession of Austria. The cloud grudgingly drifted away in September of that year as Britain, France, Italy and Germany signed the *Munich Agreement*, in effect protecting European countries from further aggression. Relief was short-lived, however, for in March 1939, Hitler, with scant heed for his 'agreement', invaded and annexed the Czech lands, Bohemia and Moravia.

Britain and France, suspecting that Hitler's territorial ambitions had not yet been fulfilled, and anticipating that his next target would be Poland, promised their support in that eventuality. Young men aged twenty-one and twenty-two were invited to volunteer for war service. Many did, in the spirit of adventure.

Teaching was my chosen profession and at the end of session 1938–39 having said farewell to the Senior 3 class I taught in Camlachie Primary School in Glasgow's east end, I dutifully accompanied my parents on holiday to the Isle of Arran. A second holiday, however, was in prospect as Ian, my future husband, had invited me to meet his parents and spend the last two full weeks of August with them at their home in Tarbert, Argyll. Ian, too, taught in Glasgow, but we had first met in Tarbert when I was on holiday there in my student days.

On Saturday, 12 August 1939, I travelled to Tarbert by train and steamer and when finally the picturesque little fishing village came into view its sun-drenched shores radiated an air of charm and tranquillity. Yachts slid effortlessly into and out of the harbour and as the steamer drew close to the pier the tanned faces and limbs of those standing there bore testimony to the fact that the weather clerk had indeed smiled kindly upon them. For some, the holiday was over: others were waiting to welcome families or friends, and there were those who had come simply to watch the steamer arrive and depart ~ with perhaps not a little curiosity about new arrivals!

Tarbert Harbour

As I waited to disembark I caught sight of Ian on the pier and his raised hand indicated that he had seen me too. A taxi took us to *Bonawe* and a warm welcome from Ian's parents ~ much to my relief, I confess. From that moment, for me at any rate, Hitler and his Nazi accomplices ceased to exist.

During the first week of the holiday we golfed, played tennis, swam and sailed amid glorious weather. We also attended a dance in the village hall which, although billed for 8 pm only came alive some three hours later. Everyone participated but the local appetite for Eightsome Reel, Strip the Willow and Dashing White Sergeant far exceeded that of summer visitors who, perhaps like me, were more in tune with the gentler terpsichorean delights of Glasgow's Plaza Ballroom where the centrepiece was a sparkling fountain and the band played the latest hits.

On the second week of the holiday, as the sunshine unbelievably continued, we pursued similar outdoor activities. On the evening of Thursday, 24 August, however, we fulfilled a promise to baby-sit for Ian's sister and her husband. Innocents that we were, we fondly imagined that the baby girl would sleep soundly until her parents returned. Not so! A whimper, that grabbed no attention, in time became a crescendo whose peak could not be ignored. We lifted her from her cot and thereafter we were left not only holding the baby but entertaining her too. She gurgled contentedly as we sang all the nursery rhymes known to us. She demanded an encore. We wilted with exhaustion but summoned up sufficient energy to switch on the wireless to hear the 9 o'clock news, for reports were circulating that a highly dangerous situation was fast developing in Europe. In sombre tones the news reader delivered this chilling message:

> ### Here is a special announcement:
>
> *In view of the present situation, the Ministry of Health issues the following warning:*
>
> *It is desirable that teachers from schools in evacuating areas should return to their schools on the morning of Saturday, 26 August. The Government wishes to emphasise that this is not a notice that evacuation will take place. If evacuation should become necessary, full notice will be given and everyone concerned will be told what to do.*
>
> *The possibility of putting an evacuation scheme for school children into operation depends, as is well known, on organisation by school units under the charge of their teachers. Teachers are key-men and their attendance at their posts, like that of other key-men, is important under the circumstances.*

At a stroke, the cosy, carefree world in which we had been cocooned disintegrated. We waited impatiently to be released from our baby-minding and when at last we were, we hurried back to *Bonawe*, packed up our belongings and made ready for an early start the following morning.

We travelled to Glasgow by bus, a seemingly interminable journey during which we had little to say to one another, wondering instead what the future, if any, had in store. On reaching Glasgow we went our separate ways, having agreed to meet after school on Monday, 28 August, at Glasgow's favourite rendezvous, *The Shell*, in Central Station ~ if nothing untoward had happened in the meantime.

On the morning of Saturday, 26 August, I reported to Camlachie School as requested. All but one of the staff were present as the headmaster, Mr Murdo MacRae, briefed us on Government plans for a possible evacuation of children from crowded city areas likely to be targeted by enemy bombers. Camlachie came into that category and for such an undertaking a rehearsal was obviously necessary. This was arranged for Monday, 28 August.

The rehearsal went ahead as planned and at a staff meeting afterwards we were asked to report the next day for normal classes. Normal classes? The undercurrent of excitement made concentration impossible and it seemed as if the school day would never end. But when it did, I boarded a tramcar which took me to the city centre where I met Ian, only to discover that he was no more enlightened than I was.

We walked the short distance to the Paramount Picture House Café where we caught up with other teachers of our acquaintance, and over coffee there was only one topic of conversation and little optimism.

In school the days dragged on and on, press reports keeping everyone on tenterhooks.

Wednesday 30 August

PEACE OR WAR?

Thursday 31 August

CRISIS NEAR ITS CLIMAX

On that day, at 1.30 pm Mr MacRae received a coded telegram confirming that evacuation would take place. Nevertheless news headlines on Friday, 1 September, ~ **LAST EFFORTS FOR PEACE** ~ seemed to suggest that all was not yet lost but almost simultaneously Hitler's armies were invading Poland, sending tanks, supported by dive bombers, thundering across the border. On the same day the first of the evacuees left Glasgow. Camlachie children were not among them but staff were asked to report to school at 9 am the following day, Saturday, 2 September.

When I arrived at school a notice had already been posted on the school gate advising that evacuation would take place the following day. Staff, pupils and participating parents were asked to assemble in the playground at 7 am. Each person must carry the gas mask previously provided, take the minimum of luggage and some food for the journey. Quite suddenly I felt strangely intoxicated by an emotional cocktail of relief (that the waiting was almost over), apprehension (about the outcome and consequences of war) and sadness (over separation from family and friends).

That night sleep eluded me, fearful that I would have difficulty getting transport at around 6 am ~ especially on a Sunday. I need not have worried. Trams were running and I arrived at school in good time as did all other staff members.

When details relating to our departure had been checked and rechecked we straggled along the route to Parkhead railway station, rehearsed barely a week ago, this time with a cardboard box containing a gas mask slung over our shoulders, a label attached to our clothing and each person carrying some sort of holdall. A few mums with under-school-age children and one mum who was expecting a baby in the Spring of 1940 had also chosen to participate in the evacuation scheme.

When we reached the station we found that the train was already waiting for us. Non-participating mums and dads were forbidden to enter the platform so there were some tearful goodbyes as they hugged their offspring and watched from a distance as the youngsters boarded the train in family groups previously arranged.

When all were aboard, for safety reasons a porter locked the door of each compartment so we were cut off from our fellow-travellers, but the implications of this arrangement did not immediately register.

At precisely 8.30 am with a loud hiss of steam the train pulled out of the station, and so began a long, long journey to a secret destination.

LMS (London Midland and Scottish Group) operated on the west coast route to Scotland and LNER (London and North Eastern Railway) operated on the east coast route.

CHAPTER 2

The Longest Day

The children in my compartment, fourteen of them, quickly settled down as travelling by train was a new experience for almost all of them. Partings were at least temporarily forgotten and the atmosphere became more like that of a school outing than a wartime evacuation. Near-hysteria arose, however, when the first train travelling in the opposite direction thundered past at alarming speed and terrifying proximity.

There were many unscheduled stops on the way as our train was all too often shunted into sidings to allow swift passage of war material or troops. At first this gave the impression that we had reached our destination but in time we became resigned to the reality that we had not. Indeed, after seven long hours we were still locked in our compartments, the food we had brought for the journey long since consumed.

About 3.30 pm our train stopped at a large station, the name of which had been erased as had the names of all stations. I recognised this one as Perth and lowered the window hoping that we had at last arrived. Heads popped out from every compartment window and there was no mistaking the fact that we were all expecting the station porter to unlock the doors. Instead he informed us that Britain and France had declared war on Germany and also that we had still further to travel. My plea that we might be released from our captivity for just a few minutes was sympathetically but understandably refused. So far we'd coped with the embarrassment of travelling in a train without corridors and consequently without water and toilets. Heath Robinson would have been proud of our remarkable inventiveness when the need arose!

Considering the restrictions of a railway compartment with no seats to spare, the day so far had passed reasonably well but although we sang songs and played all manner of guessing games, there is a limit to patience. The youngest children became weary and kept asking, as children do, "When will we be there?" and "Will we soon be there?" I had no answer. I neither knew where 'there' was nor how long it would still take to reach it.

The motion of the train and the thrumming of its wheels on the track eventually had a soporific effect on the youngest travellers. The others seemed content to sit quietly but no doubt thoughtfully. We all knew that war had been declared but strangely enough no-one commented.

For me, the pressure to keep boredom at bay was at least temporarily allayed. We were travelling through some of our country's most beautiful scenery where fields, trees, wayside flowers and hills bore the signs and lovely tints of autumn ~ purple, red, brown, orange, yellow and myriad shades of green, all enhanced by brilliant sunshine.

Inner thoughts, however, began to intrude, diverting my attention to the contrasting scene we had left behind. There, drab tenements flanked the cobbled streets. Our grey stone school buildings were sited on the very edge of a busy thoroughfare, Gallowgate, where trams rattled past on one side of the school and trains on an overhead railway thundered past the upper windows on another. Adjacent to the school buildings was a cooperage, with hammering a constant source of noise, while from time to time a most unpleasant odour would assail our nostrils. Indeed, an entry in the school's log book (12/1/36) recorded a further hazard.

This afternoon rooms became unbearable due to smoke from a fire in the adjacent cooperage.

I shuddered to think how our Glasgow eastenders would react to peaceful rural surroundings. Would they know how to behave? I recalled the sprays of flowers kindly gifted to me in school, in my innocence receiving them graciously until one pupil enlightened me of their source. She had seen the donor remove them from the 'gravey' which, I discovered to my horror, was the nearby Janefield Cemetery.

Our travelling folk ~ the Codonas, Smiths, Wilmots and Whites ~ came to mind. They were children who, with their parents, left Glasgow in the Spring of each year to tour the country with their Fairground Attractions, returning in the Autumn to winter in their caravans in the nearby site reserved for them ~ Vinegar Hill, 843 Gallowgate ~ and prepare for the annual Christmas Carnival in Kelvin Hall. This year when they returned we would be gone. What would become of them?

Questions raced around in my head as if they were on skates but I quickly dismissed any possibility that parents and children left behind might not survive the expected air raids on the city. That was too awesome to contemplate.

About 4.30 pm the speed of our train noticeably decreased. Was this yet another siding or could it possibly be that we were at last reaching our elusive destination? Tension mounted. In anticipation we roused the sleeping children and from our compartment windows we saw a crowd of people, necks craned, looking anxiously in our direction. Surely we must be 'there'.

The train shuddered to a halt as if, like us, wearied by its long journey. Excitedly we gathered together our assorted belongings. Meanwhile a porter was unlocking each compartment door and we all spilled out into glorious fresh air and golden autumn sunshine. We were indeed there and reunited with our fellow travellers. As usual, the name of the station had been erased but a man, who introduced himself as Provost Haggart, stepped forward to say, "Welcome to ABERFELDY!" Unfortunately, at the same time a swarm of bees decided to give us a warm welcome too, halting proceedings and terrifying the children who lashed out at them with gas mask containers, bags and anything else that came to hand. In spite of warnings about the consequences of such behaviour and the impression it would convey to the local people, the battle continued until eventually the bees conceded defeat, took off and peace was restored.

The billeting officer, clipboard in hand, then took over. He explained that arrangements had been made to accommodate the children as families and that Camlachie staff might like to assist in allocating them to appropriate households. The children would be pupils of the local school, Breadalbane Academy, and teachers would be members of the Academy staff. Camlachie's school accommodation would be in the Town Hall, a short distance from the Academy building.

The following information was recorded in the school's log book.

At 2.30 pm on 31 August 1939, the school was closed to prepare for the arrival of war evacuees from Glasgow and, by the order of the Education Committee, remained closed for teaching purposes until 15 September 1939. The evacuee children, though not all of them, continued as pupils in the Academy until the date of their return to Glasgow, 16 October 1943. For the term of their stay the local staff had the help of five teachers lent by Glasgow Education Authority.

Perhaps it was the incident of the bees that inspired a local ten-year-old pupil to contribute the following article to the Academy's magazine.

The Evacuee

He was a trim little fellow, the evacuee. Accompanied by his wife he had arrived at his new home in the early days of the war.

Smart and alert in all his ways, it was plain from the high way in which he carried his head that he was a wee fellow full of self confidence and not free from pride.

One look at his fiery eye revealed that the evacuee was one whose temper was not to be trifled with. Many and fierce were the battles he had to fight before he claimed the honour of being the champion local figure.

Now his cup of happiness is full, and his pride knows no bounds as he struts beside his bantam wife and her brood of tiny chickens.

(M.M.)

CHAPTER 3

New Homes

Parents with pre-school children were billeted first. An unoccupied but furnished house, conveniently situated, had been prepared for them, and a member of the evacuation committee accompanied them there. Thoughtfully a supply of basic foods had been provided.

The process of billeting was a lengthy one but if the children were apprehensive they didn't show it ~ of course they were exhausted and totally mesmerised. Not one showed reluctance to go off with strangers, not even John who might have been expected to protest. Instead he went meekly with the Provost who had gallantly offered to take 'the wildest boy'.

Camlachie staff were last to be billeted. The headmaster and senior members of staff were first in line and in due course my colleague, Emily, and I were told that we would be billeted together. We could hardly believe our good fortune when we discovered that we would be living in a house called *Woodside* which was almost opposite the Town Hall. The billeting officer accompanied us there and introduced us to our hostess, Miss Haggart, a genteel, silver-haired lady who greeted us somewhat nervously saying, almost apologetically, that she had never before had 'lodgers'. Other members of the household to whom we were introduced were her brothers, Johnny and Peter, both veterans of the First World War (1914–1918) in which Peter

had lost an arm. In spite of his disability, however, he was an expert and well-known salmon fisher with many fishing tales to tell, given the slightest encouragement!

An attic bedroom had been made ready for us and we followed our hostess up two flights of stairs to our room where we unpacked and had a quick wash. A china ewer with matching basin had been provided along with a large jug of hot water. Supper was ready so we wasted no time in going downstairs for it. To say that we felt hungry would be a gross understatement.

We were shown into a room at the front of the house which served as both dining and sitting room. A graceful oil lamp with a pretty glass bowl gave comforting light but there was no evidence of any other source of lighting. The table, with a pristine white tablecloth, was set for five people. We sat round it and grace was said by Johnny (as it was before every meal, we subsequently discovered).

The sound of the door bell intervened just as supper was about to be served and Miss Haggart rose to answer it. We heard a man's voice ask to speak with one of the evacuee teachers and, as the elder, I went to find out if there was a problem.

It was the Provost and he was greatly dismayed as he explained how his evacuee, John, had climbed out of an upstairs window and was sitting on the roof of an extension, resolutely refusing to go back inside. I had no knowledge of where the headmaster or any of the other members of staff had been billeted so, much as I had looked forward to that supper, it would have to wait until the unusual difficulty had been resolved.

On the way to the scene of the trouble Provost Haggart described how he had run a bath for John who, the minute he saw what was happening, opened the bathroom window and quickly disappeared outside.

When we reached the house, there was John still sitting defiantly on the extension roof. Daylight was fading.

"What on earth are you doing out there, John?" I called up to him.
The answer was immediate, "He's gonny droon me!"

I couldn't believe it. John was a streetwise eleven-year-old who had always portrayed himself as a tough guy but now he was near to tears. I felt sorry for him.

It took a great deal of gentle persuasion and much explanation that there was no intention whatsoever to drown him before he could be convinced, possibly by my assurance that I would remain in the house till the bathing process was over. He seemed to take some small comfort from that for he grudgingly left his outpost and crawled back inside, muttering to himself all the while.

As I waited, I reflected on the home John had left behind. It was well nigh impossible for him to understand this strange new world into which he had been catapulted. In Glasgow he lived in a 'single end' ~ a house of just one apartment. There was no bathroom, only an outside toilet shared with other people in the tenement building. Personal washing would be done in a sink, but supervised spray baths were available on the school premises. Clothing would be taken for washing to the 'steamie' (a public wash-house).

Here was John, in a large villa that must have measured up to his concept of a palace, alone with two adults who were total strangers to him. Their intentions he didn't trust. Their refined language he certainly wouldn't understand, and the domestic equipment would be completely unknown to him. Small wonder he was in a state of culture shock. It was obvious that he was unlikely to settle down and anybody's guess as to what he would be up to next.

The bathing was completed without further fuss and I have to say that the Provost and his wife handled the matter with remarkable *sang-froid*. I felt sorry for them too.

As I made my way back to *Woodside*, darkness was falling. Street lamps were unlit and householders were fixing their blackout curtains, blinds or window frames to ensure that no light whatsoever escaped to guide enemy planes. This was a Government order that came into force on 1 September 1939 and which applied to the whole of Britain. Wardens patrolled the streets to ensure that the order was being obeyed, and failure to comply carried a fine or jail sentence. A warning was usually given for a first offence. Blackout restrictions initially caused a number of accidents as people bumped into walls, lamp-posts and other people: inadvertently stepped off pavements or tripped over them, and fell or cycled into rivers. I was thankful indeed that there was just sufficient light to enable me to avoid an encounter with the River Tay as I wearily retraced my steps to *Woodside*.

Back there after what seemed like two days rolled into one, the much-needed supper became a reality. The others had eaten and were anxiously waiting to discover if my mission had succeeded.

Our hosts were, I'm sure, relieved (at that moment anyway) that they had been allocated two young women teachers and not a headstrong eleven-year-old boy.

After I'd had supper, Emily and I asked to retire for the night so, for the second time that evening, we followed Miss Haggart to the attic bedroom. She carried a small, lit, oil lamp which she left for our use, and she insisted, in spite of our protests, that she would bring breakfast to our room in the morning, a luxury to which neither of us was accustomed.

We flopped into bed and into oblivion and I certainly knew nothing more until a knock on the bedroom door the following morning signalled that breakfast was being served as Miss Haggart entered carrying a tray with toast, boiled egg and tea for each of us. War? I hadn't given it a thought! Nor, I'm sure, had Emily.

It is worth recalling here that John's dislike of bathing was not entirely unique in Aberfeldy. The late Dr. N.D. MacKay, in his book *Aberfeldy Past and Present*, 1954, humorously recounts the following incident:

> A tinker of my acquaintance had just got his discharge from
> Logierait Poorhouse, in the days when it was a Poorhouse.
> At the gate he was met by another who, some time before,
> had spent a few days in the same institution. Said the second
> to the first, anxiously,
> "Did they gie ye a bath?"
> "Aye," answered the first with a shudder.
> "Gosh!" exclaimed number two in an awestruck whisper,
> "An whit did ye think o't?"
> "Man," was the earnest reply, "A'd often heard tell o' a
> bath but dod! A never kent it was sic a bluidy awfu' ordeal!"

From Glasgow's eastend to Perthshire's hills, river and fine houses

CHAPTER 4

New Environment

Clear blue skies and brilliant sunshine heralded the early autumn day as Emily and I stepped out from *Woodside* and crossed the road to the Town Hall on Monday, 4 September. It was a far cry from my daily ten mile bone-shaking journey by tramcar from Airdrie to school in Glasgow ~ and was it really only one day since our departure from Camlachie?

Mr MacRae and some of the staff were already there and shortly after, when everyone was present, the rector of Breadalbane Academy, Mr Balfour, arrived to show us our allotted school rooms and offer any assistance required. He explained that accommodation in the Academy building, which normally housed both primary and secondary pupils, was already overstretched by the enrolment of evacuees who had come privately, from areas outwith Glasgow, to stay with relatives or friends. As a consequence, the secondary commercial classes were now rehoused in Breadalbane Church Hall and two primary classes had accommodation in the Town Hall. There were sufficient rooms for us but it meant that more than one class would have to be contained within a single room.

Apart from rooms used as classrooms, another room in the Town Hall had been allocated for use as an ARP (Air Raid Precaution) centre, where wardens were on duty on a rota basis day and night to receive telephone warnings if enemy planes were in the vicinity. A siren, positioned on the roof of the Town Hall, would be activated if a 'red alert' were received. It emitted an eerie wailing sound, we discovered, loud enough to inform the whole town. Hearing it proved to be a spine-chilling experience, especially when it sounded during the night. As our bedroom was opposite, there was not the remotest chance of sleeping through 'Moaning Minnie' as we christened it, and we listened nervously for the drone of planes, dreading the worst, and heaved a sigh of relief when the 'All-clear' signal sounded its long, high-pitched note and the danger, whatever it was, had passed.

Layers of sandbags shielded the lower windows of the Town Hall as a protection against splintering glass should bombs be dropped. So, even in our rural surroundings we could not escape the sights and sounds of war.

Our pupils, complete with gas masks, began to arrive. They seemed glad to see us, their link with home. Some of the younger children were a bit tearful, but for that first morning tears were soon forgotten, sunshine wonderfully creating a feeling of well-being.

John was last to arrive, not at all tearful but certainly truculent and almost hysterical as he informed us that he was 'definitely gaun hame'. He didn't like *the big hoose, the grub, the bath, the quiet.* His opinion of his hosts he kept to himself ! Mr MacRae calmed him down, then having checked that all our evacuees were now present, the task of distributing pupils to the allotted school accommodation began.

Not much, if any teaching was done that day. Intervals were staggered and pupils played happily and safely in the sunny courtyard while staff unpacked books and stationery and rearranged seating which consisted of wooden benches, so high that the smallest children had to be lifted on to them. Blackboards had been provided but the one in the room I shared with two other members of staff sat on top of a gas cooker. It was the strangest day of my entire teaching career, but what a lot of work and thought had gone into preparing for our arrival!

Back at our billet when school was over for the day, Emily and I had 'afternoon tea' with the family, following which Johnny showed us round the garden, his pride and joy. In the back garden there were trees with ripe, mouth-watering plums. The branches of apple and pear trees hung low with the weight of the fruit they bore. Beyond the fruit trees was the vegetable garden with potatoes, leeks, carrots, turnips and onions to be used to make nourishing soups in the winter months ahead. The fruit was there for the taking ~ if you could stand the bees. Surplus apples and pears were to be preserved in glass jars or made into jam. And wasn't that fortunate! Sugar was rationed in January 1940. It was almost as if the warm autumn weather had been granted to provide abundance for the intense cold we were later to experience.

Having viewed the garden, Emily and I set off to explore the small town. Shops were mainly in and around *The Square* and it seemed possible to buy almost anything we would need. There were two cafés and a Picture House, several churches and banks, and a post office where I bought stamps. A little further on from the post office, on the opposite side of the road, the now familiar name *Haggart* appeared above a large, imposing shop which, we later discovered, was owned by the Provost. The window displays showed a range of exclusive tweed clothing and accessories. It would be difficult, one would imagine, for such a business to survive during wartime, especially when clothes' rationing was introduced. But this firm, founded in 1801 in the small village of Acharn, began by buying raw wool and weaving it into tweed. Its success prompted a move to Aberfeldy where a shop, with a tailoring business, was opened. Haggart's tweeds are today marketed in Europe.

This advertisement appeared in the 1940 edition of Breadalbane Academy's school magazine. It shows the extent of their stock.

By Appointment to the late King George V.

By Appointment Woollen and Tartan Manufacturers to H.M. The Queen.

By Appointment Woollen Manufacturers to H.M. Queen Mary.

REG. TRADE MARK

P. & J. HAGGART

ABERFELDY :: Perthshire, Scotland

ESTABLISHED OVER A CENTURY

Woollen Manufacturers and Specialists of

Real Hand-Woven Scotch Tweeds and Homespuns.
Clan Tartans :: Plaids, Motor and Travelling Rugs
Home-Made Blankets and Shawls.
Ladies' and Gents' Tailor-made Sports Suits, Costumes,
Travelling Coats and Shooting Capes.
Highland Dress *(for Morning and Evening Wear)*.
Hand-Knit Hosiery, Knitting Wools, Shetland Shawls.
Also Stocks of Real Harris and Shetland Tweeds, &c.
Clan Tartans in Silk Ties, Scarves, Tam-o'-Shanters, &c.
Wools for Hand Spinning.

Send for Estimates,
Patterns and
Self-Measurement
Forms—Post Free.

We saw a notice pointing in the direction of the *Cottage Hospital* and another indicating the entrance to *The Birks*, eulogised by the Scottish poet, Robert Burns, and today a favourite tourist attraction.

The braes ascend like lofty wa's,
The foamin' stream deep roaring fa's,
O'erhung wi' fragrant spreadin' shaws,
The Birks o' Aberfeldy.

The hoary hills are crowned wi' flow'rs,
White o'er the linns the burnie pours,
And risin' weets wi' misty showers,
The Birks o' Aberfeldy.

Next we came upon a laundry. What an enterprising little community this appeared to be! Built in 1900 by James Fisher, it still exists today and vans bearing the name *Fishers Laundry* can now be seen where the firm has successfully branched out.

The original *Fishers Laundry*
Machinery was powered by steam engine for washing,
drying and finishing articles being laundered.

Our meandering took us to the River Tay and to General Wade's Bridge leading from Aberfeldy to the village of Weem and other small villages on the north side of the river. When the bridge was completed in 1735, it was the only real crossing place to the Central Highlands and it is a tribute to General Wade's engineering skills that it is still in use today, albeit with the addition of traffic lights!

At the Aberfeldy end of the bridge, on the west side, stood *The Black Watch Memorial* erected to commemorate the raising of the Regiment in Aberfeldy, first mustered on the area surrounding the monument in 1740 and unveiled in 1887.

On the east side of the bridge was a nine-hole golf course. We went into the club house where we were welcomed by 'Robbie', the greenkeeper, who offered to lend golf clubs if we wished to play. This gesture proved typical of the innate helpfulness and friendliness that permeated the whole of our stay in Aberfeldy. We learned, too, that James, one of our evacuees, had already been over the course yelling a hysterical warning to Robbie,

"Mister! Mister! The coos are eatin' yer grass!"

How very much more there is to education than mastering the 3Rs!

Back at *Woodside*, and after the evening meal, I wrote a reassuring letter to my parents, who, of course, had no idea where I was, nor had I any idea where Ian was. Shortly after, however, I received a letter from him, forwarded by my parents, telling me that he was in Neilston, Renfrewshire, from which Glasgow could be reached by tramcar! The evacuation by train had taken several hours.

CHAPTER 5

Living at Woodside

Observation on our first evening at *Woodside* that the only source of lighting appeared to be from paraffin lamps proved to be correct. Although gas and electricity were both available in Aberfeldy ~ gas since 1855 ~ our hosts had chosen not to have either, believing them to be too dangerous. We, on the other hand, having been used to gas and electrical appliances, thought that paraffin was infinitely more lethal ~ but refrained from commenting!

There was always a plentiful supply of hot water, achieved by means of a coal fire in the kitchen. The fire was part of a 'range' which had a top plate with openings for cooking pots, and an oven whose temperatures varied from very hot to cool. A gleaming black iron kettle, filled with water, sat permanently on the top plate and when boiling water was required, the kettle was either placed on one of the openings or transferred to the fire to bring it quickly to boiling point. What a weight it was!

A long-handled toasting fork hung by the fireside ready for use. Bread was speared on it and the fork held in front of the glowing coals. This made deliciously crisp toast.

Clothes' washing was done in the 'scullery' where there were two fixed porcelain basins, a deep one and a shallow one. Between the basins was a hand-operated wringer. Clothing was washed in the deep basin and vigorously rubbed on a washing board. Garments were then carefully folded and put through the wringer. After that, the clothes were rinsed in cold water and the wringing process repeated. On good days they were hung outside to dry but in inclement weather they were dried inside on a pulley.

Using the iron was initially a bit of a problem for us. It was much bigger and heavier than any iron we had used. It had a hollow casing into which was placed a metal block that had been heated in the fire. Transferring it from fire to iron with a pair of tongs was a tricky business but the iron, it has to be said, was most effective in eliminating creases.

Bella, a 'daily woman', came to help with cleaning the house for there were no energy-saving devices, and although everything was always spick and span, at the first sign of Spring a massive 'Spring Cleaning' operation began. Carpets were rolled up, carried outside, heaved over a rope and thrashed with a cane beater until the last vestige of dust had been expelled. Heavy curtains were removed from their hooks and sent to the laundry. Drawers were emptied and re-lined with fresh paper. The chimney sweep came with his brushes, climbed on to the roof and brushed the soot down into the fireplace which had been covered over to prevent soot spilling into the room. Nothing was wasted. The soot was spread over the soil in the garden to enrich it.

Emily and I did no housework but we did our personal washing and ironing. Sheets, pillowcases and tablecloths were sent to the laundry. We washed and dried dishes and did some light shopping. Bulky items were delivered to the house.

We were free to come and go as we pleased. We had expected to be given a door key but soon discovered that doors were locked only at bedtime and last in locked up. That task usually fell to us!

In retrospect, it must have been a traumatic experience for three elderly, unmarried people, set in their ways, to have two strangers of a different generation suddenly thrust into their well-ordered household. Nevertheless, after the initial shock they seemed to take it in their stride and I think that they quite enjoyed having us. We were never addressed by our forenames but gradually formality was avoided by referring to us as *Fairie* and *Darkie*, representing our respective hair colouring!

Miss Haggart was always concerned that we should have sufficient food 'of the right kind'. Neither Emily nor I had been used to having a cooked breakfast and certainly not one served up daily in bed. We suggested, in the nicest possible way, that tea and some of her crisp toast would be ample, but the very idea that we should set off for school without a 'proper breakfast' appalled her and she would have no part in it. The alternative was porridge, the family breakfast, but we had both expressed a distaste for that.

By the end of September we had each consumed twenty-seven boiled eggs. The twenty-eighth was just one too many and as we heard Miss Haggart's footsteps on the stairs Emily and I looked at one another and each knew exactly what the other was thinking ~ we simply could not face another boiled egg. But whatever could we do? We must avoid at all costs causing offence to this kindly soul. If we left the eggs in the bedroom Bella might discover them, so we took them to school with us and brought them back at the end of each school day. Soon we had collected a total of twelve eggs. Something had to be done, and quickly. So, under cover of darkness we took the much-travelled eggs to a secret place and gave them a decent burial, feeling extremely guilty for many people would have been glad of them. Eventually, however, we were able to persuade Miss Haggart to provide for our breakfast just tea and crisp, buttered toast with a lavish spread of her home-made marmalade. Delicious ~ but I doubt if she approved!

If we tired of hard-boiled eggs, the same could not be said for fresh salmon. Peter's landing skill ensured that he never returned from the Tay empty-handed during the salmon fishing season.

Not such a treat for us was jugged hare, a great favourite of the family. Neither Emily nor I had tasted it before coming to Aberfeldy but when we saw it being prepared we both had an instant revulsion to it and declined the offer to have it for lunch. Miss Haggart's argument that you never know whether you'll like it until you've tasted it, made us feel obliged to try. But my mind had been made up in advance of tasting and a sip was sufficient to justify my feelings about it. I did not like it, nor did Emily!

There was, of course, that versatile product, *Spam*, which, after being prised from its tin could be sliced and eaten with potatoes and salad or cooked vegetables. It could also be used as a sandwich filler and, tastiest of all, it could be sliced, dipped in dried egg (a wartime substitute for the real thing) and crumbs, and fried ~ if you had enough lard to coat the base of the pan.

In spite of rationing we always had sufficient and varied food to eat and it is claimed that the war-time diet was much healthier than that of the present day.

CHAPTER 6

Drama at Sea and Local Drama

There had been so much to do in our new surroundings that little, if any thought had been given to events on the war front.

The world, in fact, was in turmoil. Mussolini, the Fascist Italian dictator (and ally of Hitler), had conquered Abyssinia. Japan was endeavouring to swallow up China. Spain had been engaged in civil war ~ seen by outsiders as a struggle between the opposing ideologies of Fascism and Communism. Hitler's army was ruthlessly advancing into Poland and as Britain and France had declared war on Germany it was fully expected that the Nazis would immediately retaliate by scattering bombs over British cities. Strangely enough that did not happen.

In Aberfeldy the wireless was our main source of information and it became an evening ritual to 'listen-in'. On Sunday, 3 September, so much had been happening that the evening news broadcast was forgotten so no-one in *Woodside* heard the BBC's report that the first enemy attack had taken place, not on land as anticipated, but at sea. The transatlantic liner, *Athenia*, with over a thousand passengers on board, had been torpedoed by a German U-boat. Some time later the full horror of the disaster was reported.

On 1 September the *Athenia* had left the River Clyde to sail to Canada. Some of her passengers were people who wished, and could afford, to escape with their families to a country not at war. After leaving the Clyde, the liner sailed to Belfast to take further passengers on board. The next day she set sail for Liverpool, picking up several hundred passengers there. On 3 September the *Athenia* sailed up the Irish Sea, no-one aware that she was being closely observed through the periscope of a German submarine.

During dinner that evening the ship was torpedoed, and following the explosion the *Athenia* was plunged into darkness. Panic ensued and a mad rush to reach the lifeboats only made their launch more difficult. Distress signals were sent out and three ships responded. Three destroyers from the Home Fleet were also dispatched on the order of Winston Churchill who had been appointed First Lord of the Admiralty.

In the early morning hours of 4 September some survivors were taken to Eire and some to Greenock where they were fed and cared for by local people until appropriate hospital accommodation could be found for those seriously injured. Over a hundred people lost their lives.

Unexpectedly we, in Aberfeldy, had our own nerve-wracking drama. Mr MacRae, our colleague Fred, and I had decided that, after school when the golf course was quiet, we would walk over it with a view to playing at a future date. At a point where the course skirts the River Tay we stopped, fascinated by the breathtaking scenery. A variety of rich autumn colours clothed the steep slopes above the opposite banks. The river itself sparkled joyously in the bright sunshine as it carelessly tumbled by. Then suddenly, as we stood there, our attention was caught by something floating downstream towards us in the very middle of the river. To our unspeakable horror, as it came nearer we saw that it was the body of a small child. Simultaneously each of us made a move. I kicked off my shoes and waded up to my waist in the deceptively cold water, watching helplessly as the apparently lifeless little body floated past before I could reach it.

Mr MacRae's attempt, further down the river, was no more successful. Fred, however, with greater foresight, had gone much further along the river bank and was swimming strongly towards the middle of the river. My heart stood still as we watched him reach out and grasp the floating child, only just in time to avoid being swept away in a dangerous current.

Fred swam back towards us and as he reached the river bank we took the small body from him and laid it on the grass, now recognising the child as Wee Jimmy, one of our pre-school evacuees. Frantic efforts by Mr MacRae to revive him met with no success. Expert medical attention was required.

Leaving Mr MacRae to take care of an exhausted and bedraggled Fred, I ran with Jimmy in my arms the short distance to the main road where, by great good fortune, a large car was crossing the Wade Bridge on my side of the road. I waved down the driver, an American, and breathlessly begged a lift to the Cottage Hospital, the direction of which I had fortunately identified while exploring the town with Emily.

Although the car was apparently full, without hesitation the occupants of the back seat squeezed up closely together to let me in with my pitiful, motionless bundle, his face transparent and his lips blue and swollen.

In a matter of minutes I was telling a nurse what I knew about the rescue and giving her the little boy's name. Then, still in my wet clothing, and oblivious to all around me, not knowing whether Jimmy were dead or alive I set off to find his mum, wondering all the while what I could possibly say to her.

I headed back towards the golf course and it was not long before I caught up with a distraught mother and her expectant friend searching frantically for the missing child.

They had been sitting on the river bank, enjoying the sunshine, when suddenly they became aware that Jimmy was not beside them. It was now clear that he must have fallen, or slipped into the river un-noticed and had been swiftly carried away, under the Wade Bridge and completely out of their sight.

We ran all the way to the hospital, Jimmy's mum and I, and by the time we got there, miraculously Jimmy had regained consciousness and we were assured that he would fully recover, which he did, for after only an overnight stay in the care of nursing staff he was mercifully reunited with his family.

Next morning there was a warning to all our pupils about the danger of the river ~ all except John who was missing. A messenger to his billet returned with the news that he had left the house, presumably for school. Panic!

The police were immediately informed and in due course the missing person was identified, picked up three miles out of Aberfeldy and brought back to the Town Hall. He had 'made up his mind to walk home'!

His luck would have been out even without the intervention of the police. When spotted, he was striding out ~ in the wrong direction.

My colleagues and I were physically none the worse of our unexpected dip in the cold, fast-flowing River Tay, but the image of the floating child is indelibly engraved on my mind. It haunts me still.

CHAPTER 7

Warsaw Falls to the Germans

On Friday, 15 September, 1939, Breadalbane Academy pupils returned to
their classrooms, and by the same date, with the utmost secrecy, British army
divisions (The British Expeditionary Force) had crossed safely to France to
join their allies on the Western Front. Immediate German reprisals were
expected and Aberfeldy had a further influx of evacuees, mainly from the
south of England and not under the Government scheme.

By the end of September almost half of our Camlachie pupils had drifted
back to Glasgow. Needless to say, John was one of the departed. Those who
remained, however, were simply glowing with good health. Undoubtedly
the fine weather, regular meals and hours, and the generosity of the
Aberfeldy people had together contributed to the settling-in process and
the children's physical well-being.

Weather forecasts had been banned to avoid giving information to the
enemy, but the following report was issued on 12 December 1939 by the
Meteorological Office in Edinburgh:

```
September 1939: Dry; unusually warm 1st-9th


On the 15th a wedge of high pressure moved

eastwards over the British Isles and thereafter

a spell of anticyclonic conditions prevailed over

the greater part of the country till the end of

the month. This period was very dry on the whole;

numerous places experienced an absolute drought

from the 14th or 15th to the 29th or 30th.
```

Not everyone appreciated the drought as this gem of a poem by a Breadalbane Academy pupil clearly shows.

Summer Rain

O tardy summer rain!
How cool thy drops on hedge and tree
How welcome is thy voice to me
Thy patter on the pane.

O gentle summer rain!
Say didst thou know my fairest flowers
Were drooping in the sunny hours
Longing for thee in vain?

O kindly summer rain!
After the hot and dusty days
How pleasant are the country ways
Refreshed by thee again,

C. McD. age 10.

We, however, made the most of the fine weather with a Sports' Day and visits to places of interest, of which there was no lack. For these activities we had the voluntary help of Dr. MacKay's daughter, Annette, who was well versed in local knowledge and had an engaging way with the children. Everyone was sorry when she was called up for nursing service but by then we'd heard a great deal of the history and folklore that exists in and around Aberfeldy.

Sports' Day

Reality, however, was never very far away. Sadly, on the war front the end of September saw the gallant Poles capitulate. Defending their capital city, Warsaw, had no longer been possible. German planes had bombarded it for three days and nights. Fires were burning everywhere and there was neither water, power nor food.

The Polish army was finally driven out of Poland and into Roumania and Hungary, and although great effort to regroup was made, it was unsuccessful and Polish soldiers and airmen were distributed to different areas of Scotland, including Perthshire. Taymouth Castle in Kenmore, about six miles west of Aberfeldy, became Polish Base Hospital No.1 in Britain, and Provost Haggart's house, Eilean Riabhach, became a convalescent home for Polish soldiers and airmen after they were discharged from Taymouth Castle. The Provost's house had been requisitioned before the war began (as it had been during the First World War) but he and his wife were rehoused locally by the time we arrived.

Soon we began to hear at first hand of Nazi atrocities in Poland, particularly against Jewish people, and we learned some unpalatable facts about the power and ruthlessness of the Nazi invaders. But it was not until the final days of the war in Europe that the full horror of Nazi brutalities unfolded.

Throughout October the number of Camlachie evacuees continued to decline. Decreasing hours of daylight posed a problem for both evacuees and their guardians. People of all ages, however, were being urged to get busy with their knitting needles to provide warm winter garments for those serving in the Forces. Wool, knitting needles and patterns were available from the WVS (Women's Voluntary Service) so the girls joined the knitters. Permission to use a small room in the Town Hall was granted and we made a start. The older pupils knitted mitts and scarves while the younger ones knitted squares to form a blanket. These sessions took place twice a week in the early evening, and because of the blackout the children were escorted to their billets when the sessions were over.

For most of October the weather continued to be fine. The Met.Office later reported:

> A marked feature of the month was excessive sunshine, but snow was reported from high level Met. stations in Scotland on eleven days.

By the end of the month Ben Lawers was sporting a white cap ~ not one we had knitted! Was winter about to fan us with its icy breath?

CHAPTER 8

New Friends, Old Friends

At the end of November, 1939, Mr MacRae and senior members of staff returned to Glasgow to restart the education of those Camlachie pupils who did not register for evacuation and the now considerable number of pupils who had gradually drifted home. Parents of some of the remaining evacuees thought that, as it was safe for staff to return, it was safe for their children too. Their departure left us with just fifty Camlachie pupils, but of course there were also evacuees from outwith Glasgow. Only four of the Camlachie staff remained ~ Emily, Anwyn, Fred and I ~ Fred going to the Academy building to teach secondary pupils while I became 'Teacher-in-Charge of the Town Hall Evacuees'.

Emily, Anwyn and I worked as a team and I had their unstinting help and also the loyal support of the rector, Mr Balfour, who visited us daily in spite of the increasing demands on his time.

All our pupils were then accommodated in one very large room in the Town Hall and as well as teaching pupils at three levels, each with different abilities, and preparing the top level pupils for their 'Qualifying Exam' (The Quali!), I had many extraneous duties. Endless forms had to be completed relating to admissions, departures, attendances, progress reports, medical and dental care.

A number of our Glasgow evacuees received free clothing and footwear which, when required, had to be requisitioned from Glasgow Corporation.

Other Glasgow evacuees, who had been billeted in outlying villages, began to trickle into the Town Hall school as their teachers were recalled to Glasgow where there was an acute shortage of teaching staff. The newcomers settled in well to their new surroundings and soon felt, as the rest of us did, that they were truly part of the local community.

Adult friendships had been formed through church, golf club, badminton club, choir and ARP duty for which we volunteered. The ARP room in fact became an evening gathering place when table tennis was installed.

Camlachie pupils made new friends too. Denominational and non-denominational children were taught together and there were no social class divisions.

Staff v Pupils Annual Golf Match

Although new friendships were formed by teachers and pupils, it was necessary to maintain links with homes and school in Glasgow and before Mr MacRae left Aberfeldy it was agreed that we would keep in touch by letter with Camlachie parents and pupils, and they with us.

Unknown to us, Mr MacRae had sent some of our letters to one of His Majesty's Inspectors who had visited Camlachie in the summer term before evacuation took place. The following acknowledgment was forwarded to us.

12/3/40.

Dear Mr MacRae,

I was very interested to have your letter and learn something of Camlachie activities in and out of Glasgow. Mr King, Miss Leitch, and I enjoyed reading the children's compositions and think that your scheme is most praiseworthy.

The internal evidence of the letters points to very successful work on the part of your staff in making their pupils happy and contented — heartening these days when one hears so many 'evacuation tales'.

Looking forward to my next visit to Camlachie,

Yours sincerely,

James G. Strachan.

The 'evacuation tales' referred to in the letter concern press correspondence in which complaints were made in respect of (a) poor billeting arrangements and unsuitable accommodation for evacuees arriving in some reception areas and (b) evacuees unsuitably clad, unclean, sometimes verminous and carrying infectious diseases when they arrived to be billeted. These reports prompted a debate in the House of Commons in which the MP for Camlachie, Mr Campbell Stephen, had this to say:

> I think that the movement of hundreds and thousands of women and children has been a colossal achievement, a tremendous operation carried through without any previous experience. Like everybody else I pay my tribute to teachers and to the people in the reception areas, and to the mothers...
>
> As a Member of Parliament, I have travelled about the country a great deal and I make bold to say that the people of Glasgow are as decent, clean and respectable as one finds in any country town or in any other part of the country. I believe there has been a tremendous amount of exaggeration in connection with this matter...
>
> I believe that the people in the reception areas are kind to the evacuees. We are all very much alike, and if people take others into their homes it creates discomfort for them and it means they are showing a spirit of generosity.

I can speak only for the Aberfeldy billeting arrangements which were superb in every way. Our pupils did not have the sartorial uniformity which, in these days was the prerogative of those in fee-paying schools or schools sited in predominantly middle-class areas. When they left Camlachie on 3 September 1939 all of our pupils were clean. Confinement in a packed railway compartment for eight hours with no access to water guaranteed that neither pupils nor staff arrived at their destination with shining morning faces. Nor should it be forgotten that, when evacuation began, children were at the end of a two-month holiday period. For the underpriveleged, where fathers were often unemployed, the time was mostly spent playing in the streets or back courts.

I will never forget my shock and disbelief when, in my first year of teaching, I visited a Camlachie pupil recovering at home from an appendix operation. He was one of a family of nine children who, with their parents, shared only one room of modest size. The floor was bare and weeds grew up through it. The only evidence of sleeping facilities was a recessed bed, so where did they all sleep and how well? How did each member of the family find his or her own clothing each morning and get to school on time? That pupil was always personally clean (as was his unironed clothing) although there was no running water in the house. The visit was an enlightening experience. To know is to understand.

CHAPTER 9

Unexpected Encounter

With snow creeping further and further down Ben Lawers, and petrol rationed (September 22), Fred decided to sell his car which he had now brought from home. Before doing so, however, he suggested that we should see some of the outlying villages known to us only by name through class registers of attendance.

A Sunday was chosen for the outing and Fred, Anwyn, Emily and I set off immediately after lunch. Fred took the road across the Wade Bridge, through the Poplar Avenue, then west to Weem where we stopped to have a quick look round.

The Camlachie evacuees insisted on calling this avenue of trees *The Popular Avenue*.

From there we passed Castle Menzies which, reputedly, Bonnie Prince Charlie visited in 1746, then on to Camserney, Dull and Coshieville where a small hotel offering afternoon tea tempted us inside.

Our order was quickly taken as there was only one other person in the dining room ~ a rather serious-looking young man who seemed preoccupied and paid no attention whatsoever to our arrival.

While we waited to be served we chatted among ourselves, commenting on the distance some pupils had to travel daily to school in Aberfeldy and the likelihood of their being snowed up in winter. Instantly the lonely figure came to life, calling out to ask if we were evacuee teachers. When we answered that we were, he said he was, too, so Fred invited him to join us, which he did with alacrity, and thereafter his tale of woe unfolded. He had been married in July and had bought a house in Giffnock (Renfrewshire). His wife was now living alone there while he languished in a remote corner of Perthshire with, not surprisingly, only three Glasgow evacuees remaining.

My mind went into overdrive. Giffnock... Renfrewshire... Neilston (quite near) ... would an exchange of teachers be possible? I felt sure that Ian would welcome it as his letters to me betrayed just a suspicion of envy of my Perthshire location. The secondary department of Breadalbane Academy was seriously understaffed due to the continuing enrolment of evacuees who came privately... if the three outlying pupils were transferred to the Town Hall and billeted in Aberfeldy...

Initial hesitation to give voice to these thoughts, for fear of raising false hopes, was suddenly abandoned. I threw caution to the winds and offered my possible solution. Needless to say it was taken up with considerable zeal. Some discussion followed, after which there was an exchange of personal information and it was agreed that my only role in this intrigue would be to seek Mr Balfour's approval the following morning, and take it from there. We said our farewells, having spent much longer in the hotel than we'd intended, and set off on the next part of our journey.

Coshieville is situated at a junction where the road north leads to Kinloch Rannoch and the road south to Glen Lyon. Fred chose the latter but decided there wasn't time to go up the Glen so he drove to Fortingall where the famous yew tree stands by the churchyard and is reliably reported to be well over 3000 years old. Legend has it that Pontius Pilate was born in Fortingall but this is apparently without foundation.

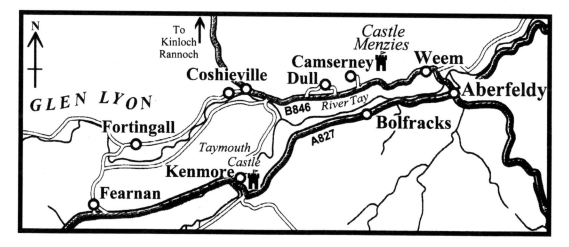

Before the war, Taymouth Castle had been a hotel.

From Fortingall we proceeded to Fearnan then to Kenmore where we had
our first view of Taymouth Castle. The circular tour was completed by way
of Bolfracks and from there back to Aberfeldy.

The following morning I informed Mr Balfour of our outing and the
unexpected encounter, making known to him what had transpired. Without
hesitation he gave his approval but reminded me that Glasgow's Education
Department would have the final say. He felt, nevertheless, that there was a
strong case for a positive response as all concerned would apparently benefit
~ not least the secondary department of Breadalbane Academy!

Within a week Ian arrived in Aberfeldy and three new evacuees were
enrolled in the Town Hall school. Ian was billeted in the small Guest House
where Fred was living. Both had been accepted on condition that should the
war continue until Easter, they would find alternative accommodation as the
Guest House was fully booked for the holiday period. The war, of course,
did continue beyond Easter and Ian and Fred were accommodated in Struan
House overlooking The Square.

When Ian reported to Breadalbane Academy a time-table had already been
prepared for him, and like the rest of us he quickly adjusted to his new
surroundings.

CHAPTER 10

Leaving Nothing to Chance

Censorship of news was now strictly in force so broadcasts neither reported action that might be useful to the enemy nor information that might lower the morale of the British people. Listeners therefore began switching to a German wireless station broadcasting from Hamburg.

"Germany calling," drawled the voice of the announcer, William Joyce, nicknamed Lord Haw-Haw because of his highfalutin accent.

The purpose of these broadcasts was to weaken the resolve of the British public by reporting false information. Listeners, however, were not easily duped and tuned in rather for the programme's entertainment value than for information which, in any case, was taken with the proverbial grain of salt.

The reality was that no bombs had yet been dropped on British soil. On the continent of Europe, the British Expeditionary Force had not fired a shot. Instead, our soldiers were helping their French allies to extend their defences ~ the Maginot Line between France and Germany ~ to include the border

between France and Belgium. People called it *The Phoney War* and many thought that it would be over by Christmas.

We, in the Town Hall, wondered if it were really necessary to continue carrying our gas masks daily. How we all hated gas mask drill! We'd started by wearing the masks for just five minutes at a time, gradually increasing the agony to half an hour, by the end of which I could scarcely breathe, and the plastic window had completely steamed up, making the pupils in front of me invisible. They, of course, fared no better. Nevertheless it would be wrong if we were lulled into a sense of false security because of lack of action on the western front so we persevered with the drill despite the discomfort.

If nothing seemed to be happening on land, it was a different matter at sea even if we didn't hear about it from British reporters. While at anchor in Scapa Flow, a stretch of deep water within Orkney's southern islands, one of our great battleships, the *Royal Oak*, was torpedoed and sunk by a German U-boat. Over eight hundred crew members were lost.

The Germans had also been laying mines in British coastal waters, and since the beginning of the war many of our merchant ships had been sunk. It was hoped, of course, that we would be starved into submission.

Suddenly there was a marked lowering of temperatures in Aberfeldy and Ben Lawers' white cap had quite considerably extended. Camlachie evacuees had already received their allocation of Corporation winter wear, and where this did not apply, foster parents dipped into their own pockets and bought warm clothing for those children whose parents had not made provision.

School staff were in need of warmer clothing, too, so visits to Glasgow were planned. My mother had earlier taken a day trip to Aberfeldy, ostensibly to bring me clothing more suited to falling temperatures but arguably with an ulterior motive ~ to satisfy herself that my claim that all was well was fact, not fiction!

Emily and Anwyn went home first, on a Saturday, and Ian and I set off the following Saturday, leaving with an early morning train so that we could return later the same day. Our journey to Glasgow was uneventful but on arrival there were many reminders that the city was on a war footing. Everyone appeared to carry a gas mask but it was claimed that the content of the cardboard box was quite likely to be the owner's lunch!

Baffle walls had been erected at the entrances to tenement buildings. Sandbags were piled round shop doors and windows. Barrage balloons, strategically placed, floated above the city to discourage low-flying enemy aircraft. Many people were in uniform, and military vehicles, some driven by women, were much in evidence. I felt a stranger in the city I had known so well and had left so recently.

We went our separate ways, Ian to his digs in Hyndland and I to Airdrie, having agreed to meet at Buchanan Street Railway Station fifteen minutes before the departure time of the train we had chosen for the return journey.

When I reached home I found my grandmother there too, busily knitting air-force-blue socks for our neighbours' son, a navigator in the RAF. When I commented on the quality of her work she said, "Just imagine, these socks could be flying over Germany." She seemed pleased that, at eighty plus, she was making a small contribution to the war effort. Sadly, the handsome young navigator was killed in action over Germany, one of many of my contemporaries to meet a similar fate before the war was over.

After the shock of seeing so many signs of war in Glasgow, I was pleasantly surprised to find that in my parents' house everything appeared quite normal. The lunch my mother had prepared showed no sign of shortages. My favourite foods were there as a token of welcome. Indeed, blackout curtains were the only evidence of constraint. Conversation for the most part revolved round life in Aberfeldy but I was also eager to hear home news as I had completely lost touch with all my friends.

All too soon it was time to find, and change into, warm clothing and also pick up items that would be useful to me in and out of school ~ books, music and my badminton racquet. I left with a promise to visit again during the Christmas holiday period and travelled to Glasgow by bus. From the bus terminus I walked the short distance to the railway station where Ian was waiting for me and, as we made our way to the platform from which our corridor train would leave, we were confronted by posters asking, "IS YOUR JOURNEY REALLY NECESSARY?"

Travel by civilians was discouraged so it wasn't surprising that we had little difficulty in finding seats. There was, in fact, only one other person, a lady, in our compartment so I elected to sit by a window and Ian sat next to me.

A short time after the guard had blown his whistle and the train had moved off, the door from the corridor to our compartment opened and an expensively dressed, black-coated, squat little man, carrying a brief case, entered and sat down opposite me. There was something indefinable about him that made me feel uneasy and I found myself repeatedly and surreptitiously glancing in his direction.

As soon as we had passed the unmarked Stirling station, which I recognised, he leaned towards me and asked if I could tell him the name of the next station. His guttural pronunciation convinced me of what I had suspected ~ that he was not British ~ and I answered truthfully enough that I didn't know, as did Ian. He did not enquire of the lady traveller nor did she volunteer information but almost immediately he hurriedly left the compartment.

The train slowed as it approached the station and we saw a number of men in civilian clothing standing at intervals along the platform. As soon

IS YOUR JOURNEY REALLY NECESSARY?

TICKETS

RAILWAY EXECUTIVE COMMITTEE

as the train stopped, almost at once our compartment door was opened and a man glanced all round. No questions were asked. He closed the door and quickly moved on.

The lady traveller made no comment, nor did we. Was she known to the man? Was it coincidence that he chose this compartment? Or was she, as we were, paying heed to such wartime posters as 'Careless Talk Costs Lives.' and 'Be like Dad, Keep Mum.'?

We were curious to know what happened to the man in black but could only hazard a guess that he was a spy, one that had not earlier been identified by the Intelligence Services. Thousands of men and women suspected of being enemy agents or Nazi sympathisers had been rounded up at the start of the war and would be interned for its duration. Italian café proprietors, highly respected in the communities in which they lived, were interned too, but released when it was established that they posed no threat whatsoever.

Back at school on Monday morning I was met by two excited little girls. They also had been on an excursion on Saturday. Their foster parents had taken them by car to Perth to be kitted out in green kilts, woollen jumpers, warm stockings and sturdy shoes. Small wonder the girls were so anxious to show them to me. Their winter school wear would otherwise have been the regulation navy jumper and gym tunic which marked them as needy.

Below is a picture of the house where the girls stayed ~ *Freiceadan Dubh* (The Black Watch) ~ aptly named as it overlooked the Black Watch War Memorial.

CHAPTER 11

Towards the End of 1939 and the Beginning of 1940

British summer time had officially ended on 14 November and there was then greatly reduced afternoon daylight as clocks were put back by an hour.

By the end of the month, Russia's Red Army, on the order of Stalin, had attacked Finland. But the Finns, like the Poles, fought bravely to defend their country. Bitterly cold weather and heavy snowfalls proved to be to the Finns' advantage as, camouflaged in white, and fighting on skis, they sniped at the Russian soldiers who were poorly equipped for the intensely cold weather.

That was no more than an item of news, far removed from Aberfeldy. We had snow, too, not in great quantities, just sufficient to transform the landscape, and as December appeared on our calendar, thoughts turned to Christmas, a strange new Christmas for the Glasgow evacuees.

With great enthusiasm we rehearsed a Nativity play and rigged up costumes and props. We made Christmas cards and decorations, lustily sang carols and practised games and dances for a Christmas party. And what a lovely surprise we had! Mr MacRae sent the handsome sum of £1 for a Christmas treat for the Camlachie evacuees and Mr Balfour joined us in some of our festivities.

When the first school term was over, Emily and Anwyn left to spend Christmas with their respective families. On their return, Ian and I spent a few days with my parents. Naturally, parents of our Camlachie evacuees were anxious to have their children home during the break too, especially as it seemed perfectly safe to do so. Once home, however, the family spirit prevailed and a number of our evacuees failed to return to Aberfeldy. A letter sent to me from Mr MacRae confirmed that they had again enrolled in Camlachie school.

The month of January, 1940, brought further snowfalls and an intensity of cold such as I had never before experienced. Few of the Glasgow children had seen snow lying for any length of time. In the city, when snow fell it was quickly rendered to a horrible, dirty slush by traffic and pedestrians. Here, in Aberfeldy, the snow was crisp and now fell in such quantities that roads were blocked and trains had to be dug out from drifts.

A train in Scotland being dug out from a drift

Icicles hung from buildings and trees. Ponds froze ~ to the delight of curling enthusiasts, of which Johnny was one. It was he who introduced us to the sport of outdoor curling at Pitilie and I still visually recall the first glimpse I had of the frozen pond nestling among trees, the moonlight filtering through their branches to the glassy surface. Still ringing in my ears are the excited calls, "Soop 'er up! Soop 'er up!", as team players brushed the ice vigorously with their brooms.

Met. Office reports later confirmed the intensity of the cold.

```
January 1940: Exceptionally cold; intense frost;
considerable snow during the latter half of the
month.
The month will long be remembered for the intense
cold. Over Scotland as a whole it was the coldest
month since 1895 and the coldest January since
February 1838. Snow was widespread and the falls
considerable in the latter half of the month. In
Scotland snow lay undrifted to a depth of a foot
in many places while drifts caused trains to be
marooned and villages isolated. Sunshine exceeded
the average on the whole.
```

The Camlachie children had a wonderful time as they experienced the exhilaration of sledging, snowballing and building snowmen. It mattered not that Aberfeldy was cut off and vehicles had to be dug out from drifts.

Europe, too, was in the grip of one of the coldest winters on record, a blessing in disguise, undoubtedly deterring the enemy from risking an attack on the western front.

I started the year the proud owner of a fur coat, a Christmas present from my parents. Not only did it keep me warm out of doors, but it served also as an extra bedcover, for the attic bedroom in winter felt like an ice house.

Each evening Emily and I filled a 'pig' (china jar) with hot water. Before retiring for the night we put our pigs in the bed we shared. They were very comforting while they kept warm but it was a different story if we fell asleep without removing them and our feet suddenly came in contact with them. Ouch!!

At the beginning of January, ration books had been issued to everyone and it was necessary to register with a grocer. Every adult was entitled to a quarter of a pound of butter, bacon and sugar per week. By then, however, the *Woodside* larder boasted an imposing array of jars containing jams, jellies and preserved plums, and boxes of apples and pears, all of which were greatly enjoyed and much appreciated.

CHAPTER 12

On the War Front the Situation Changes

On 1 March, 1940, Breadalbane Academy pupils staged a concert in the Town Hall. The evacuees were invited to take part and contributed three dramatised nursery rhymes.

On 11 March, Anwyn was informed that she could no longer be retained in Aberfeldy as evacuees from outwith Glasgow now exceeded those from Camlachie school.

As well as a departure, however, there was also an arrival when a baby girl was born in hospital to our expectant Glasgow mother. Announcement of the birth greatly relieved the anxiety of some local ladies, for the sight of this evacuee mum, with large frontal protuberance, waddling serenely through the town as she did her shopping, had raised eyebrows and set tongues wagging. Such was the concern that she might go into labour at any time ~ or worse, at any place ~ that the local doctor felt obliged to alert me to their fear. Did I know exactly when the baby was due? Of course I didn't but the information I had was that the birth was not expected for about eight weeks. Eight weeks? Incredible! Surely it must be twins and it would therefore be advisable to have her taken to Murthly Hospital for tests.

Now, the sight of heavily-pregnant women in Glasgow's eastend was no rare phenomenon and they always seemed extremely laid back about their 'condition' so I was not at all surprised that our mum-to-be thought a hospital visit quite unnecessary. By now, however, seeds of doubt had been sown in my own mind and I began to have worries about the validity of the eight-week forecast so I decided to broach the subject again.

Tentatively I suggested that, as she was away from home, perhaps she should have tests, and with an air of 'Anything for a quiet life', she relented.

Tests showed that she was indeed carrying only one baby which would be due in approximately eight weeks' time, and of course the baby girl duly obliged.

To my surprise I was invited to carry her to church for her christening so on a bright Sunday morning I walked to the house where the evacuee families lived. The infant was already dressed in a long white christening robe and wrapped in a cosy woollen shawl and as I lifted her and cradled her in my arms I felt very nervous indeed about my ability to carry her safely to the church.

Just before we left the house, I was given a small, neatly-wrapped parcel containing a 'christening piece' to be handed to the first person we met on the way. It was claimed that this would bring good fortune to the recipient and also to the new baby ~ a custom with which I was not familiar.

From the point of view of carrying a baby, I was thankful that the church was relatively near, but on the other hand as we stepped out into the street, and found it completely deserted, I became increasingly concerned that we would reach the church with the 'piece' still in my possession. However, just within sight of the church building, a door opened and a lady stepped out. She seemed to be taken aback when I offered her the small parcel, but when an explanation was given, she accepted it graciously, so that was one thing less for my fertile imagination to cope with!

On arrival at the church we were shown into the vestry. We heard the congregation singing a hymn, towards the end of which we were ushered into the church to sit in a front pew. When the singing finished, the minister welcomed us and said a few words about the unusual circumstances of this christening. The baby's father had not yet seen his daughter. He was on active service.

I cautiously handed the baby to her mother and we walked together to the font. The impeccable behaviour of the unsuspecting child came to a sudden end when the minister sprinkled water on her forehead as he named her. She reacted with an angry yowl and continued to demonstrate her displeasure until the organist played the opening bars of *The Lord Bless Thee and Keep Thee.* Her crying then immediately ceased but there were more than just a few moist eyes among the congregation.

When the ceremony was over and we had left the church, we were surrounded by people waiting in the grounds, eager to have a peep at the baby who seemed delighted with all the attention.

We then returned to the family billet. Wee Jimmy, his mum and the baby's sister were already there. A lunch, that included a christening cake, had been prepared. The east end of Glasgow seemed a million miles away. Had I, like Alice, fallen down a rabbit hole and entered a fantasy world? It seemed like it but, as always, there lurked a sharp reminder that we were a nation at war.

In the month of April, Hitler struck again, this time invading and over-running Denmark, then Norway. The Norwegians fought gallantly for their country but a British force that landed in Norway to give assistance had to be withdrawn for lack of air support.

On 8 May, following a House of Commons debate, Prime Minister Neville Chamberlain resigned, and on 10 May he advised King George VI to send for Winston Churchill who would form a new government.

On 10 May, the day Churchill took up office as Prime Minister, Holland, Belgium and Luxembourg were invaded by the Germans. Bombers struck at airfields, and parachutists floated down, seizing bridges and destroying defences. Within the space of five days the conquest of Holland had been achieved.

British and French troops moved forward to assist the Belgians, but lacking sufficient tanks, guns and ammunition they were no match for the advancing German army. On 27 May the Belgians sought an armistice. Meanwhile the Germans had broken through the French lines near Sedan, forcing British troops to retreat to Dunkirk where they were well and truly trapped.

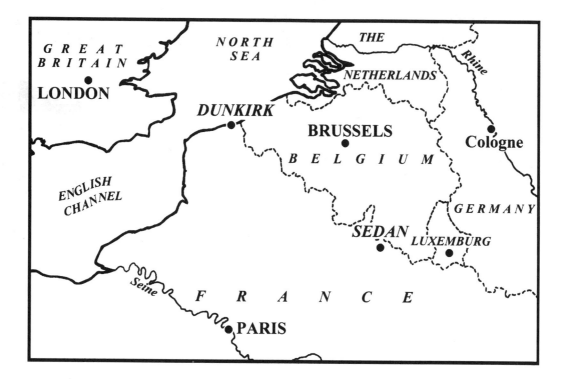

A call went out for immediate help to rescue the beleaguered troops whose chances of surviving the German onslaught seemed slim indeed. The response was magnificent. Hundreds of people who owned small boats in the Thames estuary and south coast ports immediately responded to the call, and others from further afield joined them as soon as possible.

It was a strange armada of fishing boats, paddle steamers, tugs, yachts, life-boats ~ in fact any vessel that was deemed to be sea-worthy ~ that crossed the Channel, a distance of 70 miles, assisted by ships of the Royal Navy and given air cover as they made the desperate crossing to Dunkirk and back, many times over ~ a mission that seemed doomed to failure.

The evacuation of Dunkirk

It was dark when the first flotilla of small boats had cleared the English coast, but soon a glow from the town of Dunkirk, in ruins after continuous bombardment by German planes, enabled crews to see other boats around them and so avoid collision. A pall of dense smoke from burning vehicles also worked in their favour, screening them as they approached the French coast.

On the Dunkirk beaches, British and Allied troops, exhausted and injured, waited to be rescued. For many, their hopes were realised. The deafening sound of guns and exploding bombs did not deflect crews from the mission they had undertaken.

At sight of the approaching boats, weary troops staggered to the water's edge and waded out to waiting craft, and in the course of a week, despite constant attacks from the air, almost 225,000 British troops and over 112,000 Allied fighting men, many of them badly wounded, were returned to British soil. Guns, transport and equipment had to be left behind in France.

In Parliament, Winston Churchill described the rescue as 'a miracle' and vowed:

"We shall go on to the end... we shall fight on the beaches; we shall fight on the landing grounds; we shall fight in the fields and in the streets; we shall fight in the hills; we shall never surrender."

On 10 June, Mussolini declared war on the Allies and attacked France from the south. On 14 June, Paris fell to the Germans, and two days later the swastika was flying from the Eiffel Tower. The French, whose armies were in total disarray, asked for an armistice which was signed on 21 June 1940. From Norway to the south of France the coastline was in enemy hands. Britain stood alone.

Winston Churchill called a highly secret meeting of his War Cabinet at which he unveiled plans to transport Britain's wealth to Canada. If invasion did take place, Churchill had no intention of conceding defeat. Money would be available to continue the war from outside Britain.

It was an immense gamble, for ships crossing the Atlantic ran the risk of being attacked from the air by the Luftwaffe as well as being torpedoed by U-boats or blown up by mines. The Cabinet nevertheless agreed that it was a risk worth taking and on 24 June, under the greatest secrecy, a convoy of ships set sail from Greenock with a cargo of gold bars and investments owned by private citizens. Against all the odds the ships arrived safely in Halifax where a special train was waiting. The precious cargo was transferred to it during the hours of darkness and whisked off for safe keeping. During July and August similar transportations were carried out without the loss of a single ship and in spite of the huge number of people involved on both sides of the Atlantic, not a word of this clandestine operation was leaked.

CHAPTER 13

On with the Show

With the threat of invasion now becoming a reality rather than a remote possibility, it was difficult to keep thoughts from straying in that direction. In the last few weeks of a summer term it is unusual to begin new projects but Emily and I thought that, in the circumstances, we must devise some means of diverting attention from affairs in Europe.

Always Striving for Excellence was Breadalbane Academy's motto. Camlachie did not have a stated motto but an intention to aim always for 'the best', supporting one another in our efforts. For instance, a member of staff who was a skilled pianist, accompanied the choirs during practice time for Glasgow's Annual Music Festival. Others helped by travelling to the Festival with the choirs and supervising the children before and after their performances.

As part of the Academy ~ and we were encouraged to feel part of it ~ we thought that we would not let the side down, so to speak, if we staged a small-scale concert of our own. Performances at the Music Festival had earned for Camlachie School choirs Certificates of Distinction which were framed and proudly displayed in the school hall for all to see.

Sir Hugh Roberton's adjudication remarks were a worthy incentive to continue musical training with the children. We took on board his criticism and, as the marking sheets show on *pages 56–57*, improved performances were the result.

THE GLASGOW MUSICAL
FESTIVAL ASSOCIATION.

_____ Festival.

VOCAL ENSEMBLE Marking Sheets

PROFICIENCY		A	B	C
Tone Intonation Accuracy Blend, Balance Technique Articulation	50	42	42	
INTERPRETATION				
Imagination Rhythm Phrasing Words Style	50	44	43	
		86	85	

171 TOTAL

Class No. 4   Entry No. 13

Competitor _Camlachie School, Glasgow_

Test Pieces.

A "As I sat on a sunny bank" - arr. E. Sharpe

B "Windy nights" - Stanford

C _____

NOTE.—Details underlined need attention

80 is to be regarded as the standard of a good average performance.

A

Not bewk please (I know its difficulty).
Slow pace. Quite right if you feel it this
way. Sweet unforced tone. A perfectly
lovely last verse, & the descant so

B

beautifully done. I consider this way
a fine achievement. .

PROFICIENCY		A	B	C
Tone Intonation Accuracy *(Blend, Balance) Technique Articulation	50	43	43	
INTERPRETATION				
Imagination Rhythm Phrasing Words Style	50	44	45	
		87	88	

TOTAL 175

Class No. **4**   Entry No. **8**

Competitor ____ Camlachie School, Glasgow.

Test Pieces.

A Sleeps the Noon.   (Songs of the Hebrides)

B One more River. (any five verses) J. Bateson.

C _____

NOTE.—Details underlined need attention

80 is to be regarded as the standard of a good average performance.

A Most touching in its simple beauty What a labour of love to set these lovely vowels in _music_ + other words. We liked this greatly. It has at its best a note of quiet rapture that held us.

B Smart, + controlled, + all so happy. Conductor's ideas here saved it

C fault; + she does not fuss, or try to make her songs do what they can't do.

Hugh Robertson *Adjudicator*

On two successive years, letters were received from Marie S. Irving, visiting music teacher to Shawlands Academy. She was quite unknown to us, but in her first letter to the school she said that she had tried to congratulate the children on their festival performances but got a row from an attendant! The second letter contained a 10/- note, in those days quite a fortune, so the children were thrilled.

Glasgow, S.2. 3/5/39.

Dear Miss McCall,

I think I have a surprise for you. It certainly was to me.

I mentioned to my Headmaster, Mr Peter McDougall to-day, how splendidly Camlachie had done last night and at once he pulled from his pocket the enclosed 10/ bill which he ordered me to send to you. I think I told you Camlachie was his first School.

Now you can have a beano and I hope the children will have a jolly good time. They deserve it.

I am yours sincerely
Marie S. Irving.

We now set about planning a programme of entertainment based on items that had been part of our Arts' curriculum ~ music, including an operetta, Scottish country dancing and a play, *The Bishop's Candlesticks*, an adaptation from *Les Misérables*.

Our plan, when presented to the rector, was applauded and we were offered use of the main Town Hall for rehearsal and performance. Admission would be free but proceeds from a collection from the audience would be donated to the *Knitted Comforts Association*. Mr Balfour would address the audience at the start of the programme.

Time was short and although the items did not require much rehearsal, they had not been performed in costume. We decided that they should, and with the willing help of foster parents and others we successfully staged our little show and raised £20.

Here we are in our Town Hall classroom planning the programme. The picture on the right shows Mr Balfour addressing the audience.

Some Items
from
the Show

Before the term ended, however, the ever-increasing threat of a Nazi invasion brought a further influx of evacuees, mostly to the senior primary classes and mainly from Edinburgh, Dundee, and the south coast of England. It was, of course, too late to include them in our programme but we invited them to get together to write a little play of their own. As is evident from the photos, they got together ~ separately! They provided their own costumes and gave an open-air performance for the established evacuees, and wasn't Hitler now terrifyingly close at hand!

Heil Hitler!

What a swell party!

61

CHAPTER 14

Hitler Threatens to Invade

Although our contracts as evacuee teachers did not stipulate that we should remain in Aberfeldy during school holidays we decided that, under the present circumstances, we should not abandon our pupils.

Hitler had carefully planned his conquest of Britain and was utterly confident of success. First he would target British ports and shipping. Next he would attack our airfields and rid the skies of the RAF. Then he would terrify the civilian population by dropping bombs on their cities. Finally he would send his barges and airborne forces across the English Channel. He hoped that the first two parts of his plan would cause so much alarm that the British people would beg for peace ~ on his terms ~ and he would then head a triumphal procession through an unscathed city of London.

The people of Britain, however, were not sitting idly by, waiting for this to happen. Along the entire eastern coastline concrete blocks covered the beaches and barbed wire and gun emplacements were set up. Piers were detached from the shore and church bells silenced, to be rung only in the event of an invasion.

Airmen from Canada, Australia, New Zealand and Rhodesia arrived in Britain to join British and Polish pilots. Women were called on to volunteer for war work such as making munitions, joining the *Land Army* to work on farms: joining the *WVS* for a variety of duties including driving ambulances and other vehicles: doing clerical work and preparing and serving food in canteens. Those with nursing experience were also asked to volunteer for service.

In response to an appeal for Local Defence Volunteers, subsequently called The Home Guard, men of all ages signed on ~ including Ian and Fred. At first they wore civilian clothing and carried any implement with which they could defend themselves if they came under attack. Later, khaki uniforms were issued and members were trained in the use of firearms.

Lectures were given at evening classes to prepare volunteers for whatever would be required of them in the defence of Britain. Teachers attended First Aid and Fire-Fighting classes where training was given in the use of stirrup pumps.

Private Ian McLullich
Black Watch Home Guard, Aberfeldy

Home Guard Defence Medal

Householders erected *Anderson Shelters* in their gardens to protect themselves from being struck by falling masonry in the event of air raids, and posters appealing to people to 'Dig for Victory' resulted in vegetables and fruit, instead of flowers, being grown in gardens.

Contrary to expectation on Hitler's part, the Luftwaffe's attack on shipping and airfields did not go as planned. During July and August, 1940, the *Battle of Britain*, as it became known, was fought in the air with unrivalled ferocity. The skill, courage and determination of our air crews demonstrated the superiority of Hurricanes and Spitfires over German Messerschmitts, and ensured our mastery in aerial conflict.

Winston Churchill's inspirational oratory played a key part in uniting the citizens of Britain and in motivating the RAF in their relentless and selfless challenge, acknowledged thus by him in a House of Commons address:

> *Never in the field of human conflict was so much owed by so many to so few. All hearts go out to the fighter pilots whose brilliant actions we see with our own eyes day after day.*

In Aberfeldy during the holiday period many red alerts were received, mostly during the hours of darkness. During daylight hours, however, there was an air of calm. On the other hand, in and around Glasgow, bombs were dropped during July, yet when the 1940–41 school session began a number of our evacuees who had been spending the summer at home with their families did not return to Aberfeldy. This deficiency, combined with the transfer of pupils who had qualified for entry to first year in the Academy, resulted in Emily's recall to Camlachie. An extra secondary teacher was sent instead. These factors alone would not have created an insurmountable problem but Ossa was heaped upon Pelion when it was revealed that some pupils from each of the undernoted schools had been privately evacuated to Aberfeldy to stay with friends or relations and would now have to be accommodated in Breadalbane Academy.

Glasgow:	Willowbank, Cuthbertson Street, Battlefield, Kent Road, Eastbank, Cloberhill, Overnewton, Park, Girls' High, Strathbungo
Edinburgh:	James Gillespie's, St Trinneans, Heriot's, Rothesay House, George Watson's, George Watson's Ladies, Craiglockhart, Edinburgh Ladies' College, Edinburgh Academy
Dundee:	High School, Lawside

The list as recorded in the Academy's log book.

Mr Balfour was now faced with the daunting task of reorganising classes to accommodate new evacuees. I was given the sub-qualifying class with well over forty pupils comprising local children, Camlachie evacuees, new arrivals who had reached that stage in their education and some children of parents who had recently come to live in Aberfeldy because of a change of work location. I remained in the large room in the Town Hall and continued as 'Teacher-in- Charge of the Glasgow Evacuees'.

The qualifying class was accommodated in a much smaller room next door and all other primary evacuee pupils were distributed, as far as possible, to appropriate classes in the Academy building. With pupils from town, country, denominational, non-denominational, state and independent schools, there was little time to dwell on the possibility of an invasion: the classroom invasion demanded immediate and constant attention and securing text books and stationery was a priority.

Aside from school affairs, having apparently satisfactorily completed a probationary period in the attic bedroom in *Woodside*, I was promoted to the large front bedroom on the first floor, with early morning room service as usual!

CHAPTER 15

A Christmas Carol

On August 31, 1940, Hitler embarked on the third part of his plan by bombing London. Churchill ordered a reprisal on Berlin. Hitler immediately responded by giving orders for *Operation Sealion* ~ the transfer of shipping to Channel ports and the invasion of Britain.

On 7 September he unleashed more than six hundred bombers, with fighter protection, in a ferocious attack on London's docks. Soon there was a raging inferno with many civilians killed or injured. An invasion now seemed absolutely certain and a coded message sent to ARP centres revealed 'Invasion Imminent'. Church bells were rung, troops and Home Guard called out and bridges blown up to limit access.

Air raids on London continued on an almost nightly basis. Glasgow, too, was targeted. On 18 September Dalmarnock Gas Works ~ a stone's throw from Camlachie ~ received a direct hit. Bombs were also dropped on Partick, on George Square in the city centre and on a school ~ small-scale indeed compared to the nightly attacks on London where civilians were now constantly in the front line.

Red alerts became more frequent in Aberfeldy but we were spared the trauma of air raids. There was no complacency, however, for invasion was another matter. The Home Guard continued its vigilance with renewed vigour. Civil Defence Volunteers passed on their expertise to new members. Fund-raising became a priority and as this was mostly a cooperative effort it was instrumental in boosting morale. A *Whist Drive and Dance* always proved to be a popular and profitable event. Concerts, too, attracted large audiences. At these functions raffle tickets were sold and those lucky in the draw received prizes generously donated by local shopkeepers.

At the beginning of October Dr Swanson, a local GP, called at the Town Hall to ask if I would undertake the production of a Christmas concert involving primary school pupils ~ local children as well as evacuees. A room in the Town Hall would be made available for evening rehearsals and as much help as might be required for costumes and props would be given by local people. The concert would be held in the main hall and proceeds from an admission charge would again be donated to the *Knitted Comforts*

Association. The proposal had been cleared by Mr Balfour so I had no hesitation in agreeing to it. Secondary staff already had their own programme for fund-raising and for providing entertainment for Polish servicemen recovering in Taymouth Castle and Eilean Riabhach. Furthermore, a mixed-voice choir was formed and conducted by the Infant Mistress, Miss Ness, and its concerts were hugely popular.

Christmas offers such a variety of material for children that there was little difficulty in providing items for an evening's entertainment. Perhaps the *pièce de résistance* of the show was the adaptation of scenes from Charles Dickens' *A Christmas Carol* ~ not least because of the spectacular gowns provided by local ladies who, with great enthusiasm, had delved into their attic trunks and had also undertaken to make costumes for children involved in other items.

A narrator introduced *A Christmas Carol* ~ 'Once upon a time on Christmas Eve, old Scrooge sat busy in his counting house.' Words linking episodes were illustrated by mimed vignettes. We had the ideal Scrooge (Bah! Humbug!) and Mr Fezziwig's Ball provided opportunities for music and dancing. The rumbustious scene where children received their presents was re-created to involve as many aspiring young actors and actresses as possible. There was no ghostly presence. Scrooge was portrayed in his nightmare as the outsider looking in on the spirit of Christmas so it was a small step to provide a happy ending.

Ian and Fred supervised the pupils who had been enlisted for stage management and they were also responsible for general discipline in the dressing rooms. Management of costumes was undertaken by the ladies who had provided them.

On the evening of the performance there was a moment of panic before the show began. One of the principal performers, Dr. Swanson's daughter, uncharacteristically failed to appear at the appointed time. Curtain-up was delayed, and just as we had decided that the show must somehow go on, a very flushed young lady was hustled into the dressing room.

"Elizabeth has German Measles," the doctor said, "but she is well enough to take part. If the other performers haven't caught it by now, they might as well get it over and done with."

Nobody did catch it but was it not ironic that, on a night when we were trying to forget the word, *German*, there it was in spite of our efforts?

A Christmas Carol

Principal Characters

Full Cast

CHAPTER 16

Hitler's Spring Offensive

Before the end of 1940, Hitler had realised that his raids on London had not made the expected impact on the British people. While not abandoning attacks on the capital, he now also turned his attention to smaller cities and towns in the belief that they would be more vulnerable.

A night raid on Coventry in November was one of the most destructive. Many people were killed and injured as thousands of houses and public buildings, including Coventry Cathedral, were completely demolished. Water mains were fractured and roads and railway lines made impassable but, typically, the stunned and weary citizens emerged defiant, firm in their determination that Hitler would not dent their spirits.

Soon it became obvious to Hitler that he could not immediately implement his invasion plans so he intensified his attacks on shipping and in January 1941 high explosive and incendiary bombs were rained on Portsmouth. This prompted compulsory registration for fire-watching duty by men and women between the ages of sixteen and sixty.

About the same time posters were displayed inviting women to join the services ~ the ATS (attached to the army), the WRNS (attached to the Navy), and the WAAF (attached to the Airforce).

Early in the New Year, the American President, Franklin D. Roosevelt, although unwilling to involve his country in war, made clear his wish to do all in his power to ensure Hitler's defeat. He proposed a Lend-Lease system whereby America would supply ships, tanks, guns and aeroplanes to Britain, to be paid for when the war was over. In a broadcast to the nation, Churchill spoke of the importance of American aid, concluding with the now famous words:

> *Give us the tools and we will finish the job.*

The agreement was signed in Washington on 11 March 1941.

March also saw the start of Hitler's Spring offensive. In the early hours of 9 March London was targeted. Portsmouth was hit on the two following nights and Brighton on 12 March. All three cities suffered many human casualties and extensive damage to buildings.

Around 7 pm on Thursday, 13 March, Ian and I set out from Aberfeldy to walk to Weem as we had been invited to spend the evening at the manse with the Rev. Ian McLellan, his wife and family. It was a glorious moonlit night and we enjoyed a brisk walk free from the hazards normally encountered in the blackout.

On arrival we were made most welcome and as the minister was an interesting conversationalist, and his wife a splendid baker, the evening passed both pleasantly and quickly, so quickly in fact that we were shocked to discover it was ten o'clock and we might have overstayed our welcome, so we hastily announced our departure.

Before leaving, however, the minister informed us that the church organist was ill. Could I possibly help out? I enquired about the organ, for the only type of organ I had played was my grandfather's harmonium. Now, a harmonium is a reed organ. Pedals operate a bellows that forces air through the reeds. It's quite hard work keeping the pedals going and failure to do so results in silence from the instrument. The minister assured me that there were no pedals. Out of sight of the congregation a church member operated a handle that pumped air through the reeds. So far, so good, but with a wry smile he added that the operator had been known to fall asleep on more than one occasion.

I felt it would be churlish to refuse the minister's request outright and agreed to try out the organ after school the following day, with Ian operating the handle.

The minister and his wife accompanied us to the manse gate and we were all surprised by an unusual glow in the night sky, far away to the west. Almost immediately we felt an unmistakable tremor underfoot ~ then another... and another... in quick succession. Obviously something terrifying was happening in the west of Scotland. It was not a time to speculate so we bade a hasty farewell to our friends and set off at a cracking pace for Aberfeldy.

Midway across the Wade Bridge we had a much more open view of the distant sky, now clearly illuminated. The tremors and persistent thudding continued. We ran the rest of the way and made straight for the ARP room which was fully manned. Neither of us was on duty that night so when it became clear that Aberfeldy did not appear to be the object of Hitler's attention, mindful that we had classes to teach the following morning we headed off to our respective billets, knowing that if the siren sounded we could be on duty immediately. Sleep was not an option for the thudding continued throughout the night as did the agonising fear that Glasgow was now suffering the same fate as London, Portsmouth and Bristol.

In the morning Aberfeldy was awash with rumours. Some claimed that Glasgow's Central Station had been razed to the ground: others that Glasgow was burning furiously following an attack of high explosive and incendiary bombs. It was difficult to know what to believe and I was greatly concerned for the safety of my parents. If we, in Aberfeldy, could hear and see what was apparently happening in Glasgow, Airdrie might well be in the line of attack.

Telephone lines were out of action so it was a trying morning in school for all of us as naturally our Glasgow evacuees worried about their families too.

By lunch time, phone lines had been restored to Glasgow city centre and I was able to speak to my father who was in his office. He assured me that he and my mother were safe and well despite having spent a terrifying night in a dark cupboard under the stairs, anticipating that at any minute they would be buried under a pile of rubble. No bombs, however, had been dropped where they lived. The devastating air attack had been concentrated on Clydeside, with Clydebank suffering the worst excesses of the blitz.

In spite of his ordeal, my father had managed to get to his place of work in the morning, to find that all other members of staff were there, too.

CHAPTER 17

Clydebank Blitz

Thursday, 13 March, 1941 was a night of unmitigated terror for those living in Clydebank. Whole families were wiped out and hundreds made homeless.

There had been what was called a 'Bomber's Moon', so fighter planes patrolled the skies: Ack-Ack guns were ready for action and ARP rooms were fully manned, for Intelligence had reported that 200 bombers had left their German bases in France and were heading west.

About 9 pm the terrifying drone of enemy planes was heard as the first wave of aircraft flew in over the River Clyde. The pattern of attack was the same as that used on English cities. Waves of German planes arrived and dropped incendiaries, lighting up the area for the main force which arrived some thirty minutes later to unleash its deadly load of high explosive bombs.

Many people had already fled to air raid shelters; others were too afraid to leave their homes when the siren sounded, but Civil Defence Volunteers were at their posts, ready for action.

Within a short space of time, telephones, electricity and water had been cut off ~ the lack of water making it impossible to quench fires. Houses, schools and tenement buildings received direct hits, killing the occupants or trapping them in the debris. Those who survived the onslaught acted with remarkable courage, risking life and limb to care for the injured and dying, in spite of interminable bombardment from the skies.

The unrelenting terror continued throughout the entire night and when daylight came and the All-clear sounded, people emerging from their shelters were confronted by unbelievable destruction. Fires were burning all around. Leaking gas mains caused many to be overcome by fumes, but those who were able dug furiously with their bare hands in the hope of finding people trapped in the rubble but still alive. Others searched for family and friends and many found that they were homeless.

By mid afternoon the following day (14 March), roads had been sufficiently cleared to allow vehicles to bring in supplies of food. By then, however, many of those who had survived had left the disaster area to stay with friends, either because they were homeless or because it had been reported that German reconnaissance planes had been detected flying over Glasgow shortly after 8 o'clock that morning.

In the early evening there was a warning that over 200 bombers were again heading back to Clydeside. When they arrived, fires from the previous night's attack were still burning so on this second night mainly large bombs and land mines were dropped ~ this time scattered over a much wider area. Undeterred, Civil Defence Volunteers, although exhausted, carried on with their tasks, and even children helped by acting as messengers.

On 17 March, not surprisingly, a large number of evacuees ~ mostly first year pupils ~ arrived in Aberfeldy from Kelvinside and had to be accommodated in Breadalbane Academy.

Before school closed for the Easter break, Ian and I had decided to stay on in Aberfeldy during the holiday period, and on the last day of term, when my pupils had been dismissed, I remained in my classroom to complete some forms relating to the Glasgow evacuees. After a short time, Kate Menzies, the qualifying class teacher, popped her head round the connecting door and cheerfully wished me 'Happy Easter'. I returned the greeting, ill-prepared for what was to follow.

Before long a secondary pupil arrived to say that Mr Balfour wished to speak to me. This was most unusual. Never before had I been summoned. What had I done, or failed to do? Was something amiss at home?

I hurried immediately to the Academy where it was explained to me that Kate Menzies' health had so deteriorated that she would not be able to return to her teaching post after Easter. In fact she would not be able to return at all. I was stunned. Never at any time had she given me the slightest indication that she was unwell, nor had I suspected that she was. That was what she had wished when she explained her health situation to the rector.

Efforts to secure a replacement teacher had been fruitless and as the welfare of her pupils, due to sit their qualifying exam in the third term, was considered of prime importance, Mr Balfour felt that the most expedient solution would be for me to take over the class. For the remainder of the school year my present pupils would be distributed throughout primary classrooms wherever there was space to install extra seating. Under such distressing circumstances there was obviously no element of choice. The suggested arrangement appeared to cause least disruption.

Part of the Easter holiday was thus spent moving personal belongings to the classroom next door and clearing pupils' desks which would have to be taken to the Academy. I was also anxious to examine the class record of work to find out what was expected during the third term.

To conclude the episode of the organ in Weem church, Ian operated the handle successfully while I tried out the double manual and the variety of 'stops', after which I agreed to play for the Sunday morning service ~ provided Ian sat beside the regular operator in case he nodded off!

Had I known then what I learned later, I might not have felt so confident that my fingering of the keyboard would produce the sound of music. Ian disclosed to me that he too had been guilty of nodding off, under different circumstances. Following two successive nights on the hill on Home Guard duty he had fallen asleep in school after setting work for his class of sympathetic sixth formers!

CHAPTER 18

All Change

Back at school after the Easter break, it was with mixed feelings that I pondered the task with which I had been confronted. I deeply regretted losing the pupils I'd taught for the past two terms, especially as the class was being split and the *esprit de corps* that had been engendered was about to be shattered. I was acutely conscious, too, of the emotive circumstances that had led to my transfer and the likely effect on the pupils. On that score I needn't have worried. Mr Balfour, with typical thoughtfulness, had paved the way by speaking with the class beforehand so, when I was called to be introduced as their new teacher, I found an unspoken, mature understanding on the part of the pupils.

The room was small, with little space between the serried ranks of desks that almost completely filled it, but I recognised before long that here was a class of over forty well-adjusted, cooperative pupils who had been extremely well taught. Their teacher had meticulously marked and graded every piece of written work done by them. Her record of work was clear and concise, stock appropriately labelled and readily accessible ~ all in spite of silently suffering an illness from which this remarkable and highly respected lady did not recover. She left to me, however, a legacy of good practice from which I was to benefit during the rest of my teaching career.

During April and May of 1941, the Nazis continued their bombing of British cities, with Liverpool on the receiving end on seven successive nights.

I, too, received a bombshell. Teaching had been a reserved occupation, but under a new Employment Order it was decreed that no man would do work that could be done by a woman. Teaching, as well as some other reserved occupations, would now be de-reserved, men called up and women aged twenty and twenty-one would require to register for work to replace them.

Under the new regulation, Ian reckoned that his age group would be due for call-up in the summer, so he had decided to volunteer for service in the RAF, his preferred branch of the British Forces. If he waited for call-up he would have no choice. There was certainly no argument against his decision. He had his medical on 20 June, 1941, and as his Grade Card shows, he passed with flying colours!

On 22 June, Hitler, with typical treachery, attacked his ally, Russia, despite the fact that he had signed a non-aggression pact. He sent in land forces, supported by aircraft, on a broad front stretching from the Black Sea to the Baltic. Churchill immediately offered help to the Russians who gladly accepted it.

By almost exactly the same date I was informed by Glasgow's Education Department that, as a shortage of teachers in the city had been created by the new Employment Order, I was being recalled to Glasgow, but not necessarily to Camlachie School. This recall did not surprise me for my monthly returns showed that, during session 1940–41, I was teaching very few pupils evacuated under the Glasgow scheme. By now, however, I was aware that, on 10 March, 1941, Emily had been sent to Innellan (Argyll), on evacuation duty and on 9 April, following an air raid on Glasgow, there had been another evacuation of pupils from Camlachie School, this time to Langholm (Dumfries and Galloway). At that moment I had little appetite for an unknown posting.

Mr Balfour offered me a permanent post in the primary department of the Academy. It was an attractive proposition but one that required much thought. First I would have to resign from Glasgow. I would also have to find alternative living accommodation in Aberfeldy as I would no longer be an evacuee teacher. Further to that, Ian had just received his Enlistment Notice for the RAF, obliging him to report for service on 22 July, 1941. Last, but not least, on 12 July we had become engaged and planned to be married in January 1942, other things being equal. That was the deciding factor.

Reluctantly, and rather sadly, I declined the teaching post in Aberfeldy. I also sent a letter of resignation to Glasgow but remained in Aberfeldy till the end of July in order to fulfil my contract with my employers. At this stage I was not at all sure what I would do or what options would be open to me.

On the eve of Ian's departure for war service we had this photograph taken. We called it *The Glums*. Of course there wasn't much to smile about.

During my last month in Aberfeldy, BBC launched a *V for Victory* campaign with a message to countries that had been occupied by Germany. The message urged people not to give in but to continue to fight for their country. It also asked them to put the V sign on any available surface, and beat the V sound using morse code •••–, whenever possible. In broadcasts to Europe the wireless station used as its call signal the opening bars of Beethoven's Fifth Symphony.

By now, The French Resistance Movement, under the leadership of General Charles de Gaulle, who had been secretly flown to England, was broadcasting to the French people urging them to resist the Nazi invaders.

In spite of death threats, members of the Movement undertook highly dangerous work. They passed on secret information, blew up installations and helped prisoners of war to escape. One of the outstandingly courageous members was 'Odette', who betrayed no-one in spite of intense and cruel interrogation by the Gestapo (German police). In 1943 she was imprisoned in Ravensbruck concentration camp where she remained until 1945 when Russian troops liberated the prisoners. She was later awarded the VC.

NATIONAL SERVICE (ARMED FORCES) ACTS

ENLISTMENT NOTICE

LABOUR AND NATIONAL SERVICE DIVISIONAL OFFICE,

44 DRUMSHEUGH GARDENS

EDINBURGH, 3.

__14__ July, 1941. (Date)

MR. __Ian F. McLullich,__

__Bonawe,__

__Tarbert,__

__ARGYLL.__

Registration No. __PKB. 4200__

DEAR SIR,

In accordance with the National Service (Armed Forces) Acts, you are called upon for service in the __ROYAL AIR FORCE   V.R__ and are required to present yourself on __Tuesday   22nd July, 1941,__ (date), between 9 a.m. and 12 noon, or as soon as possible thereafter on that day, to :—

__R.A.F. No.6 Attestation Section,__

__47B, George Street,__

__Edinburgh.__

__Edinburgh__ (nearest railway station).

* A Travelling Warrant for your journey is enclosed. Before starting your journey you must exchange the warrant for a ticket at the booking office named on the warrant. If possible, this should be done a day or two before you are due to travel.

A Postal Order for 4s. in respect of advance of service pay, is also enclosed. Uniform and personal kit will be issued to you after joining H.M. Forces. Any kit that you take with you should not exceed an overcoat, change of clothes, stout pair of boots, and personal kit, such as razor, hair brush, tooth brush, soap and towel.

Immediately on receipt of this notice, you should inform your employer of the date upon which you are required to report for service.

Yours faithfully,

J. R. M. MACKAY

for Divisional Controller.

You should take this Notice with you when you report to your Unit.

* Delete if not applicable.

N.S. 12 (5901) Wt. 18479—4180 1,000M 7/40 T.S. 677

Ian's Enlistment Notice

CHAPTER 19

Decision Time

Although it had been entirely my own choice to decline the offer of a permanent teaching post in Breadalbane Academy, when it came to the point of my departure at the end of July 1941, I struggled to contain my emotions. Fortunately the Camlachie pupils I had taught were either now in the secondary department of the Academy or had returned to Glasgow.

I had yet to decide on my course of action when I returned home. Opportunities would be few, and because of the shortage of teachers I could dismiss the idea of being permitted to join any of the women's services or train as an instructor in the GTC (Girls' Training Corps).

Once home, however, I succumbed to the call of the classroom and wrote to the Director of Education for Lanarkshire requesting an interview. A quick response gave date and time to present myself at the Education Offices where, after interview, I was offered a permanent teaching post in Garrowhill Primary School near Baillieston, just outwith the Glasgow boundary. The vacancy did not occur until mid-September so it was suggested that I might arrange to visit the school when it reopened for session 1941–42.

I was most agreeably surprised as I approached Garrowhill to see a modern single-storey building set in generous grounds with playing fields and gardens. It had been planned before the outbreak of war and built to accommodate the children of a new and expanding private housing estate.

The headmaster, Mr Hamilton, welcomed me, took me on a tour of the school and introduced me to members of staff. The classrooms were all large and bright, each with its individual pastel colour scheme. A stock room revealed an abundance of text books, stationery and large wall maps, and a store room held a variety of gym apparatus. The central hall, used for assembly and physical education, had a large stage and the luxury of two pianos.

Finally I was introduced to my new class, Primary 6. All pupils wore school uniform and rose courteously as we entered the room where an attendance board showed that there were fifty-four pupils and all were present. I was told that they were seated according to merit. Placings were made every Friday afternoon as a result of weekly tests. It was a world apart from the Town Hall school and from Camlachie, and I had almost forgotten we were at war until on my way out I saw a door marked ARP WARDEN.

With time to spare before taking up my new post it seemed sensible to start making preparations for my wedding in January. Clothing had been rationed on 1 June ~ sixty-six coupons per person for a year, not a lot when fourteen coupons were required for a woman's coat, eleven for a woollen dress (seven for a dress in any other material and the same number for a skirt), five coupons for a pair of shoes or boots, two for stockings and one for a handkerchief. I decided, therefore, that the traditional white wedding gown was out of the question and chose instead a dress and jacket that would be useful to me later.

Next on the list was finding a hotel for the wedding reception, one that had dates available in January. I had recently been a guest at the wedding of a friend whose wedding and reception were both held in Burlington House, Glasgow, solving the problem of transporting guests and wedding party from church to reception. That was my first and only port of call. A number of January dates were available and I was also given the following wartime menu for approval.

Menu

Chicken Soup

•

Roast Lamb   Mint Sauce
Chicken en Casserole
Potatoes   Vegetables

•

Trifle
Charlotte Russe

•

Coffee

•

Tea and cakes will be served later (if desired).

An additional charge of 6d per guest will be
made if tea and cakes are served.

Ian meantime had completed his square-bashing in Redcar and had been transferred to Padstow in Cornwall. Available dates were sent to him so that he could apply for leave. In due course he wrote to say that leave had been granted and 19 January, 1942, seemed to be the most appropriate date for our wedding so a reservation was made in Burlington House, a provisional number of guests given and the menu approved.

Before I had taken up my new post in Garrowhill School I was invited to be an instructor in a Girls' Club on two evenings a week. These clubs, held in schools, existed to enable adolescent girls, too young to join the GTC, to enjoy some social and cultural activities during the blackout, but when it was discovered that far more girls than expected had enrolled, a second instructor had to be appointed. We offered badminton, P.E., country dancing, music and drama and at the end of the first term musical, dramatic and dance items were presented to an audience and the inevitable collection was taken for war funds.

Early on my return from Aberfeldy I discovered that life during wartime in this part of the world was very different from that in rural Perthshire.

CHAPTER 20

Fresh Fields and Pastures New

In mid-September, 1941, I took up my permanent teaching post in Garrowhill Primary school, arriving in plenty of time as on my earlier visit I suspected that everything ran with clockwork precision. Some members of staff were already in the staffroom, the kettle was boiling and tea and coffee were on hand for those who felt the need to fortify themselves for the day's work ahead. When the 9 o'clock bell rang, however, staff on 'lines' duty beat a hasty retreat to the school entrances where pupils had lined up. Other members of staff took up their positions in the long corridors, keeping watchful eyes on the pupils who were required to walk silently in pairs to their classrooms and quietly prepare for half-an-hour's gas mask drill while homework was checked.

A timetable of work indicated that this period would be followed by quick-fire answers to questions on addition and subtraction facts, multiplication tables, tables of money, weight, length, time and capacity. The pupils informed me that Mr Hamilton regularly visited their classroom to test that they knew instantly that, for example, there were 960 farthings in a £1, 5280 feet in a mile, and 2240 lbs in a ton. Those pupils who performed less well than required were given a note to take home requesting the cooperation of parents in improving the performance of their offspring. It worked ~ even for the extended family! Some time later, William, who had been absent through illness, was brought back to school by his mother who was more anxious to advise me about her son's knowledge of *tables* than the present state of his health. She proudly announced that William now knew all his tables. The family knew them too ~ and that included William's grandfather who lived with them.

Although there was much emphasis on the 3Rs, Garrowhill pupils were by no means starved of curriculum items widely regarded as 'frills' at that time. Music, Drama, and Art featured prominently as did outdoor pursuits ~ football, netball and relay teams in which a highly competitive spirit was encouraged as was pride in their school and its well-kept grounds.

Staff consisted mainly of experienced teachers with only three of us considered the 'young fry'. But all were young at heart and the staffroom was never devoid of laughter. No-one went home at the lunchtime break which, after sandwiches and coffee were consumed, was usually devoted to correction by the upper primary staff, and preparation for the afternoon session by the others.

Mr Hamilton joined us during the morning break when relevant school matters were discussed. At lunch time and at afternoon intervals we therefore felt free to refer to him as 'The Boss' or 'J.C.' (his initials). This, of course was strictly *entre nous* so the teacher of P2 was one day surprised to see that a pupil had included in his drawing a picture of a man carrying a small attache case on which were inscribed the initials J.C. Apprehensively she enquired what the initials stood for and was somewhat relieved when the pupil promptly answered 'Jesus Christ'!

'The Boss' had names for members of staff, too. My colleague, Yvonne, and I used to rush our lunchtime correction in order to take advantage of the two pianos in the hall to play duets. Apparently this earned us the title 'Spitfire and Hurricane', the latter, I believe, assigned to me.

Firewatching was mandatory under Civil Defence Regulations but spending a night in an empty school, even with two of us on duty, was an eerie experience. Camp beds and coarse grey blankets were provided in the staffroom but sleep was virtually impossible for as soon as the light was switched off, mice scuttled about in search of crumbs for a midnight feast. Soon we decided, therefore, to firewatch in groups of four even if it meant turning out twice as often. We were then able to relieve the boredom by playing Bridge and other card games.

The ARP room was manned during the hours of darkness by a retired gentleman who made regular nocturnal excursions around the school building. He wore heavy boots and smoked a pipe from which the aroma of strong tobacco smoke choked us each time he trundled past the staffroom door.

When warnings of enemy planes in the vicinity were received we were immediately informed. We were then required to don outer clothing and dash out to the playing fields to keep watch for incendiary bombs. No matter what the night had in store, after a quick wash and something to eat we had to be ready to face our classes at 9 am *precisely!*

In this urban part of the country it was all too evident that we were at war. Food shortages were truly apparent and long queues a familiar sight. A sort of bush telegraph sent people scurrying to their local shops when someone discovered that a retailer had received an allocation of a commodity that had been out of stock. At other times the very sight of a queue acted like a magnet, drawing people to it regardless of the fact that they had no knowledge of what was on offer. The story circulated that a local man had joined a lengthy queue, only to discover, when he reached the head of it, that women's corsets were on offer!

Also frustrating were those occasions when you queued for ages in freezing weather, and found that, as you neared the head of the queue, the item was no longer available.

Shortages led to a Black Market whereby unscrupulous people offered goods at astronomical prices ~ no questions to be asked about their origin.

On the war front, the German attack on Moscow continued, but by December 1941 intense winter conditions had set in. The Russians were equipped for it: the Germans were not and were forced to withdraw as the Russians counter-attacked. Nevertheless the Germans were convinced that, when Spring arrived, they would capture Moscow.

On 7 December 1941, the Japanese carried out a ferocious and unexpected attack on Pearl Harbour, the naval base of the USA's Pacific Fleet. President Roosevelt immediately declared war on Japan, and Britain followed suit. In February 1942 Singapore surrendered to the Japanese.

In my classroom a map of the world was on permanent display. Geography lessons were never more meaningful.

CHAPTER 21

Ups and Downs

Early in December 1941, I wrote to the Director of Education advising him of my marriage on 19 January which, for circumstances beyond my control, was outwith the county's Christmas holiday period. His reply informed me that, as a married woman, my *permanent* appointment must terminate at the end of the holiday but I could be reinstated on a *temporary* basis after I was married. This appointment carried new conditions relating to pay, holidays, absences and notice of leaving or dismissal. I accepted them.

On the last day of term I suffered (not gladly!) the indignity of being 'dressed up' by members of staff, bundled into a wheelbarrow and pushed at terrifying speed round the housing estate. I had witnessed other women being subjected to such folly but never dreamed for one moment that I would be a victim. I have long since forgiven them and after all these years Yvonne (the instigator) and I are still the very best of friends.

Freed of school duties, all effort was channelled into making final preparations for 19 January, 1942. Invitations had been sent and acknowledged but not all replies were acceptances as many of our friends were on war service.

Mr. & Mrs. James McCall

request the pleasure of the company of

Mr. & Mrs. McLullich

at the marriage of their daughter

Helen Houston to Ian F. McLullich, M.A.,

on Monday, 19th January, 1942, at 2 p.m.,

in Burlington House, 183 Bath Street, Glasgow.

12 Grahamshill Avenue,
Airdrie.   R.S.V.P.

Everything appeared to be well in hand until a week before the wedding came the shattering news that all RAF leave had been cancelled as from 19 January ~ the wedding date which affected not only the bridegroom but his best man, who was also in the RAF, and my bridesmaid who was serving in the ATS. Unknown to me, however, Ian had been making a strong case for compassionate leave and a sympathetic C.O. had agreed to his travelling north on Wednesday, 14 January and returning to base on Monday, 19 January.

I immediately contacted Burlington House to explain the circumstances and ask if the date could be brought forward. Friday (not a popular day for the superstitious!), 16 January at 2 pm was offered and instantly accepted and I set about advising all our guests and our best man and bridesmaid of the change of date.

On the eve of the wedding, my parents and I were somewhat taken aback when we had an unexpected visit from our minister about 9 pm. Sadly he had come to say that my father's brother had died suddenly of a heart attack two hours earlier. The message from the family was that, although they could not be present, on no account was the wedding to be postponed. We were shocked as there had never been any indication of a heart problem.

Brightly dawned our wedding day ~ but it was fiendishly cold. Most of the guests who had already accepted our invitation, and also the best man and bridesmaid, were able to attend and the wedding ceremony was duly performed, photographs taken, the wartime meal enjoyed, speeches made and telegrams read out.

Greetings GVIR Telegram

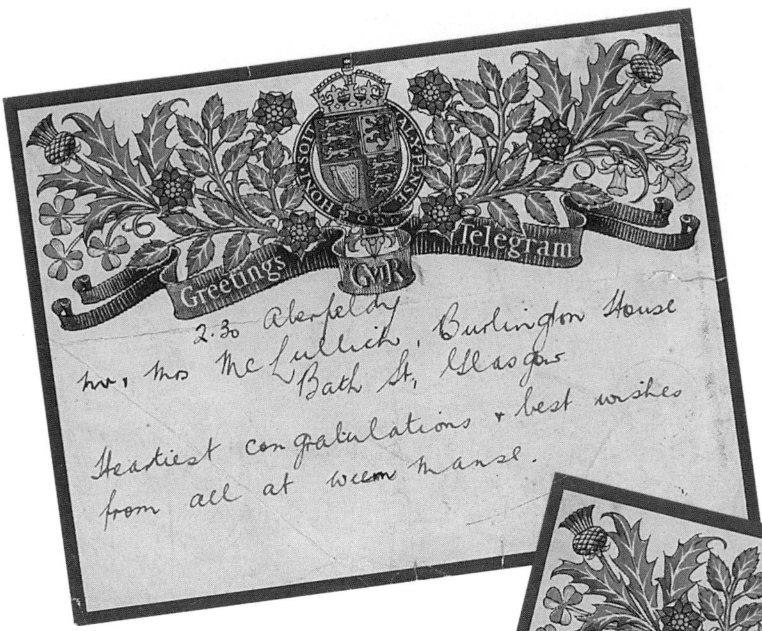

2.30 Aberfeldy
Mr, Mrs McLullich, Burlington House
Bath St, Glasgow
Heartiest congratulations & best wishes
from all at Weem Manse.

Greetings GVIR Telegram

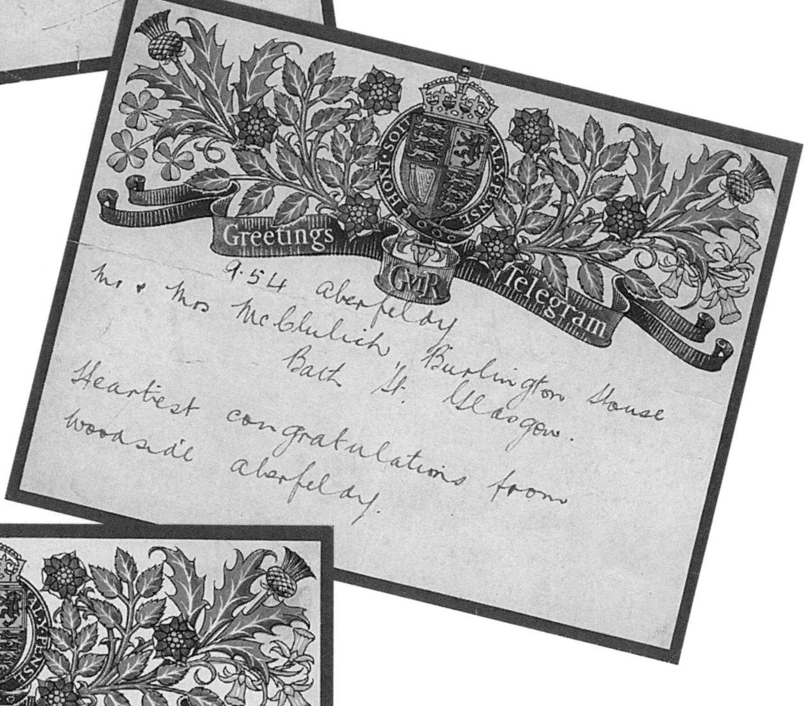

9.54 Aberfeldy
Mr & Mrs McClulich, Burlington House
Bath St. Glasgow.
Heartiest congratulations from
Woodside Aberfeldy.

Greetings GVIR Telegram

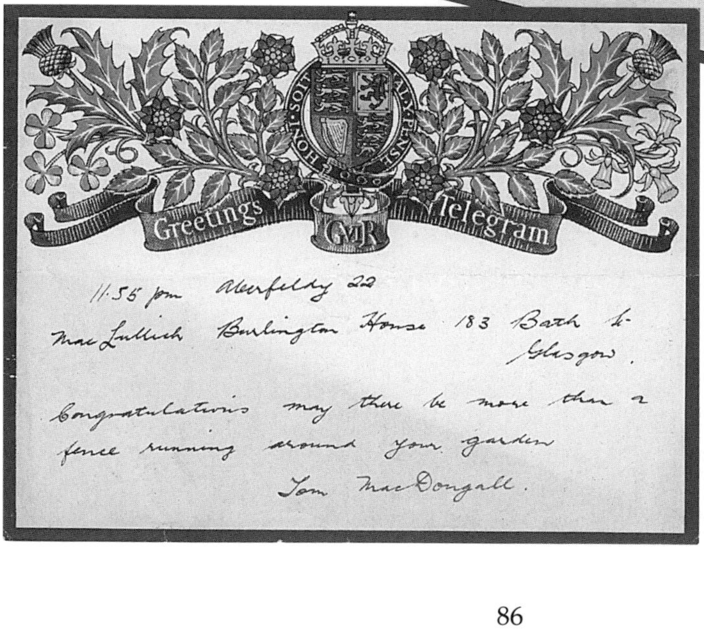

11.55 pm Aberfeldy 22
MacLullich Burlington House 183 Bath St
Glasgow.
Congratulations may there be more than a
fence running around your garden
Tom MacDougall.

The Macdonald sisters in Aberfeldy, with whom Ian and Fred had been billetted after they left the Guest House, had kindly invited us to stay with them after the wedding. This was a flexible arrangement and much appreciated. So, while our guests had tea and cakes in Burlington House, we set off by bus. The journey was far from comfortable as the vehicle was unheated and we were subjected to regular blasts of chill air as passengers mounted or alighted from the bus. On arrival, however, the welcome could not have been warmer and the world of barrage balloons, rationing, queues, uniforms and army vehicles vanished for almost two whole days.

We had wisely decided to travel back to Glasgow by train on Sunday and when we arrived at Buchanan Street station in the early evening we found that there had been a heavy snowfall which by then had reached blizzard conditions. We trudged with our luggage to the bus station where we learned that public transport had ground to a halt so there was neither bus nor taxi to take us on to my parents' home.

As we stood bedraggled in the dimly-lit bus station pondering the best course of action, a post office van stopped and the driver asked if he could help. Ian explained that if we couldn't find accommodation in the city the only alternative seemed to be the misery of spending the night in the draughty waiting room of the bus station. Perish the thought!

The driver took pity on us, and invited us to jump in, but this was not as easy as one would have imagined for the vehicle was a high one and although I was pretty agile I had to be hoisted into the cabin. Nevertheless, in spite of this rather undignified end to our wedding celebration we were more than grateful to the kindly postman who drove us to a hotel where he knew we would find accommodation for the night, and we did.

The following morning Ian caught an early train to take him back to base in the south of England and, with traffic moving again, I went home by bus to stay with my parents. The path of true love never did run smooth, it is said. Should this be true it would appear that we were certainly assured of a rosy future!

CHAPTER 22

Per Ardua ad Astra

In February 1942 Ian applied for a commission as an Education Officer in the RAF and just over a month later he received a letter of appointment, conditional on his accepting that he would be paid at civilian rates in order to comply with the Teachers' Superannuation Act of 1925. He would contribute monthly to the Superannuation Fund as would the Air Ministry. A further stipulation required that should he originate any invention during his employment in the RAF, all rights must be assigned to the Government. The former condition, *shown on the right*, safeguarded his pension: the latter seemed an unlikely expectation.

Ian accepted the appointment and in April he was dispatched to the Officers' School on Course 110, on completion of which he emerged as *Pilot Officer* and was posted to Malvern (Worcestershire). There he met a fellow-Scot who, like Ian, was a teacher in civilian life as was his wife. She had arranged to spend the May holiday weekend in Malvern and, as accommodation was still available in the small boarding house where she would stay, it was suggested, and I agreed, that I should join her and we would travel south together. She, too, was called Helen and when she wrote to me giving a description of herself and of what she would be wearing when we met for the first time, I stared incredulously at her address. The house was next to one formerly owned by my great-aunt, her husband and family.

On the evening of our departure by overnight train we met at *The Shell*. The dimly-lit station was swarming with men and women in uniform. All eyes were on the departure board and as soon as relevant platform numbers were displayed there was a frantic rush for seats on the train. Helen and I joined in the scramble and once aboard the train we trailed through the corridors till eventually we found a compartment with two vacant seats into which we wedged ourselves. We were the only civilians. All the other occupants were khaki-clad and male, and our delicate footwear had to fight bravely for floor space already almost completely claimed by heavy army boots. The atmosphere in the compartment was claustrophobic as all blinds on windows and doors were lowered and overhead lighting was

Telephone: Holborn 3434.
          Extn. 1090.
Any communications on the
subject of this letter should
be addressed to:-
     THE UNDER SECRETARY
          OF STATE,
and the following number
quoted:-
A. 372046/42//S.2.B. Ed.

24th March, 1942.

Sir,

          I am directed to offer you an appointment in the Royal Air
Force Educational Service under the following conditions:-

          1.   The appointment to be subject to a probationary period of
three months, during which it may be terminated by the department at
any time, without notice or cause assigned; thereafter the appointment
will be subject to three months notice on either side to terminate the
engagement, but the department may terminate the engagement at any time
for gross neglect of duty or for inefficiency or for misconduct on the
part of the teacher or in the event of the teacher being pronounced unfit for
further service by a Royal Air Force Medical Board.

          2.   The appointment to be subject to the acceptance of a commission
in the R.A.F.V.R. Uniform will be worn, but civilian rates of pay and
conditions of service will apply during your employment as Education Officer.

          3.   On the understanding that the signed statement of your
previous service submitted by you in support of your application on Air
Ministry Form 69 dated 18th February 1942 is correct, your commencing
salary would be at the rate of £ 303 (Three hundred and
three pounds) per annum, within the scale £234 x £15 x £480
plus a fixed allowance of £70 (seventy pounds). You would be eligible
for the first increment of £15 on 1st April, 1943.

          4.   Subject to the usual conditions attaching to the grant of sick
leave to civilians employed under the Air Ministry, sick leave on full
pay may be allowed for a period not exceeding three months in any period
of twelve months.

1557105/A.C.2. McLullich, I.F.   /5

Letter of appointment

89

barely discernible as such. Fresh air there was not and nobody spoke during the entire journey.

Soon the corridors also began to fill with service personnel who squatted on their kit-bags or stood leaning against the windows of the compartment. It seemed unrealistic that the engine was expected to cope with the weight of the bodies and luggage aboard. I was certainly thankful that I had not undertaken the journey on my own, for before we had reached our destination I was viewing the evacuation journey to Aberfeldy in 1939 through rose-tinted spectacles.

On arrival at Malvern we took a taxi to our digs. Breakfast was ready and we were ready for it. Fortunately the weekend was free of air raids, and Ian, and Helen's husband, Bob, managed some time off on both Saturday and Sunday. The weather was fine and when left to our own devices Helen and I enjoyed exploring an area with which neither of us was familiar. On Monday, our train journey home was taken much more comfortably in daylight hours.

Back at school on Tuesday morning I was shocked to find my fun-loving colleague, Yvonne, dabbing tearful eyes in the ladies' room. I knew that she was travelling to London to spend time with her boy friend, an RAF pilot, and instinctively I felt that her distress was war-related. I comforted her gently to the best of my ability.

At this time our airforce, no longer on the defensive, had taken advantage of a bomber's moon to dispatch over a thousand aircraft to the German industrial city of Cologne where, in the course of a specified ninety-minute raid, one and a half tons of bombs were dropped. That raid was followed by one on Essen where the target was Krupp's arms factory. A third raid took place on Bremen's submarine base. Inevitably a number of RAF planes did not return. The shocking news that Yvonne's boyfriend's plane was among them was broken to her at the air base where they had arranged to meet, and in due course the dreaded 'Missing Presumed Killed' followed. It is quite impossible to envisage what it was like for the many young airmen who risked their lives in the skies in the cause of freedom.

It is appropriate, however, with Yvonne's permission, to record that happier days lay ahead, and thereby hangs a tale!

In July 1943, Yvonne and a colleague, Rita, went on holiday to Oban. One sunny morning they decided to have a round of golf, in the course of which Yvonne drove a fine shot from the tee and her ball apparently landed on the fairway within pitching distance of the green. When she reached the spot where she expected to find her ball it was nowhere to be seen. A search of the rough and some ground in a nearby wooded area proved fruitless so the search was abandoned and Yvonne conceded the hole. To her astonishment, however, as she returned to the fairway, there was the ball right before her so the concession was called off, she pitched the ball to the green and holed out.

No sooner done than she was challenged by one of two young RAF officers who suddenly appeared on the scene. He (Ken) claimed that she had played *his* ball and an examination of the disputed ball proved that he was correct. A bit of good-natured banter followed and before the holiday was over they met once again after which they went their separate ways ~ but not before they had exchanged addresses.

Shortly after, Ken, a wireless operator on a Catalina, was posted to Cape Town where he remained for six months during which they kept in touch by air mail and when his stint was over and he had a period of leave, he lost no time in tracking Yvonne down to her home in Bearsden ~ appearing unannounced one day on the doorstep. He was carrying two boxes, both of which he presented to Yvonne's mother. When opened, one was found to contain two dozen eggs and the other two chickens. They were graciously accepted by the delighted recipient who had a medical condition that required her to have a light diet ~ not easy in wartime. There was, however, another box ~ a velvet box ~ which Ken took from his pocket and presented to Yvonne. When opened, the box displayed a tiny watch encased in gold encrusted with diamonds and sapphires. Yvonne was speechless (for once!) but she, like her mother, accepted Ken's gift with good grace.

By Christmas 1944 Ken was stationed in Carlisle and he invited Yvonne to spend part of her school holiday there. She agreed, but the day before leaving she developed a heavy cold and on the day of departure she felt distinctly unwell but, despite warnings from family members that she was not fit to travel, she refused to be deflected from her planned journey.

On arrival she was met by Ken who saw that her face was covered in a rash. A visit to the camp doctor resulted in a diagnosis of German Measles! But in spite of the circumstances, Ken popped the question, "Will you marry me?" Sadly for Ken the answer was in the negative.

That, however, was not the end of the story... for Ken's tenacity won the day. They were married in Glasgow University Chapel on 1 August 1946 and Ian and I were among the guests at their wedding. A son was born in October 1947.

This photo was taken following the christening. The baby is now a highly respected surgeon of whom both parents are justifiably immensely proud.

CHAPTER 23

Home from Home

Ian's service in Malvern was short term. Towards the end of June, 1942, he was posted to Prestwick. This seemed almost too good to be true and I expected I'd wake up to find it had just been a dream, or wishful thinking, but the reality dawned when I received a letter headed *St. Quivox Road, Prestwick, Ayrshire*. He had been billeted privately, within cycling distance of the airfield.

He could not have been more fortunate. His hosts, Mr and Mrs Kilgour, were the kindest of people and on their invitation I stayed with them during my two months' summer holiday from school, continuing to be amazed that people so generously opened their doors to complete strangers, to the extent of sharing their kitchen without being obliged to do so.

My limited culinary skills were certainly honed during these months for until then I'd had little opportunity to test their effectiveness. Mrs Kilgour was an excellent cook and she was happy to pass on her expertise to me and her management of food rationing.

We shopped and ate as separate families and co-operated in sharing use of domestic appliances in the kitchen which were certainly in a different league from those in *Woodside*.

Ian's working hours were erratic. He seldom had time off during the day and he frequently worked in the evenings, so I was pleased when Mrs Kilgour suggested that I might like to have temporary membership of Prestwick Ladies' Bridge Club which met on two afternoons weekly.

On several occasions I was entertained in the Officers' Mess. It was there that I first heard the Glenn Miller big band sound, imported from America by the GI's who were stationed in Prestwick. I was instantly 'hooked' by its unique harmony and orchestration of numbers such as *In the Mood*, *Moonlight Serenade* and *American Patrol*. I was not alone in feeling an almost personal loss when, on 15 December 1944, Glenn Miller's plane went missing in atrocious weather during a flight from England to Paris where his American Band of the Allied Expeditionary Force was waiting for his arrival to prepare for a concert on 21 December.

Another recollection of my stay in Prestwick was joining the huge crowd of people who followed Bob Hope and Frances Langford around the golf course. They were in Prestwick to entertain service men and women stationed there.

Ian had a wide remit but his work centred mainly on establishing and overseeing appropriate courses for service men and women whose studies had been interrupted when they were called up. Tutors had to be found for those who wished to continue their education, and the library furnished with books to meet the variety of educational needs.

Although without previous experience, he acted as instructor in making leather goods ~ handbags, gloves, wallets and moccasins ~ for those who wished a creative activity during their leisure time. The results of their labours found their way at Christmas to wives and families, and I was the recipient of a handsome leather handbag. Ian also assumed the role of 'agony uncle' to those with domestic or social concerns ~ money worries at home: husbands who, in their absence had been deserted by their wives; those unable to read or write and consequently at a loss when it came to filling in forms or making sense of letters from family or friends ~ a deficiency often adroitly concealed in civilian life. There were those, too, who could read but knew that their spelling was suspect and wished to have it checked. Rather than embarrass a writer, when Ian was completely nonplussed by what had been written, he would bring home forms to see if, between us, we could decipher the content. I clearly remember one such instance. The writer was applying for 'sick bay' because he had 'brown chastisis'. I suggested it might be an acute case of jaundice or maybe sunburn but I was assured that the man's colour was quite normal. Eventually Ian was obliged to ask where this affected the suffferer who immediately pointed to his chest and all was revealed. He had bronchitis. Why didn't we think of it?

My two months' holiday from school passed all too quickly and at the end of August I returned to my parents' home and to my new Primary 6 class. I also resumed my twice weekly evening sessions at the Girls' Club.

I was invited by the Kilgours to spend my Christmas and New Year holiday with them so I was able to participate in the seasonal festivities at the airfield. At the end of the holiday Ian gave me the good news that he had been promoted to the rank of Flight Lieutenant, then the bad news that he had been listed for an overseas posting.

CHAPTER 24

Sensing a Nazi Downfall

In the month of January, 1943, the Allies carried out a raid on Hamburg and a terrifying first daylight raid on Berlin. At the same time the Germans were in retreat from the Russian city of Stalingrad so, sensing that the Allies now had the upper hand, Churchill and Roosevelt met at Casablanca and agreed a policy of unconditional surrender by Hitler ~ no negotiated peace.

In the same month, Ian's overseas posting materialised and he was dispatched to the island of Shetland and based at RAF Sumburgh from where opportunities for leave were possible but proved to be few and far between. Still, it seemed more accessible than some other overseas postings we had envisaged.

RAF photos – Sumburgh Information Room

In March, on the home front, a National Savings Plan, *Wings for Victory*, had been launched with a target of one hundred and fifty million pounds, to be used to build bombers. Garrowhill school staff, backed by parents, were quick off the mark. A school show, which would run for three nights, was planned to take place towards the end of June, with proceeds to be donated to the *Wings for Victory* fund. A varied programme of song, dance, sketches, and recitations by pupils who attended the fashionable 'Elocution Classes' proved highly successful, attracting capacity audiences on all three nights and providing a substantial sum of money for the campaign.

Ian's first leave from Shetland was in July, 1943. He arrived unannounced, having at last managed to find space on the floor of a small transport plane bound for Leuchars. The journey by land thereafter took more than twice as long, achieved by a series of 'lifts' by van-drivers or motorists always willing to transport anyone in uniform.

I learned that, in Sumburgh, the comforts of Prestwick were sadly lacking. Sleeping accommodation was a Nissen hut, constantly damp and cold in the early part of the year. Trees looked dangerously angled on account of high winds.

Duties in Shetland were basically the same as those in Prestwick but Ian was now peripatetic as he was responsible for the educational needs of service men and women on other RAF stations on the island. For visits to these he had his own motor transport but evening journeys during the blackout, and in unknown territory, at first proved hazardous. Not much further information was imparted during his week's leave and it was only when the war was over that gradually some hair-raising experiences were verbally recalled. Indeed I was thankful that I had not known of them at the time.

Ian's next leave was not until January 1944 when he was granted seven days which fortunately coincided with my school holiday period. Within that week there were two daytime air-raid warnings during which my mother, father (now retired), Ian and I took refuge under a substantial table top ~ much less claustrophobic than the cupboard under the stairs but none the less terrifying. Shades of the Clydebank blitz and its consequences set hearts racing as soon as the drone of aircraft came within earshot. We held breath, listening for the thud, thud of bombs landing, but on both of these occasions we were spared the terrifying experience. For all we knew the aircraft we heard may have been our own.

Never for a moment did we anticipate, when we set off on evacuation duty on 3 September, 1939, that our country would still be at war in January 1944. We were now, however, beginning to see light at the end of a long, dark tunnel.

CHAPTER 25

Operation Overlord

Flushed with the success of our *Wings for Victory* show, shortly after the Christmas holiday period the possibility of staging a second show was mooted and received with great enthusiasm. Ambitious planning by staff began soon after, but this was not disclosed to the pupils who, by Easter, were clamouring for a second helping. By then we were ready to begin rehearsals and this time we had the generous offer of help from a local lady who ran her own dance school ~ *The Davie School of Dancing* ~ bringing a highly professional touch to performances.

We were not alone in making secret plans. From a base in Sicily, the American Fifth Army had crossed to Italy and after steadily advancing up the mainland, on 4 June Rome was captured. The following day a coded message to the French Resistance Movement signalled that plans for an invasion of France by the Allies were ready to be put into action and the preparatory work for landings on the Normandy coast should begin.

On the southern English coast, amphibious tanks, armoured cars, jeeps and ambulances had already been lined up. So, too, had prefabricated harbours (Mulberries), Nissen huts, and vast stores of ammunition which had been hidden in wooded areas.

The likelihood of German Intelligence being completely unaware of this huge build-up of war material was far from credible so an elaborate plan to outwit the enemy had been hatched by MI5 and it was nearing its climax.

It was fully expected that General Montgomery (Monty ~ he of the famous black beret) would be commander-in-chief of the Normandy landings but he must be seen to be elsewhere. A 'double' was therefore sought, and found, in the person of an actor, Lt.Clifton-Jones, already serving in the Royal Army Pay Corps. The great deception had begun.

He first studied photos and films of Monty then joined his staff so that he could observe every move, and note gestures peculiar to the great man himself. Finally he had an interview with Monty after which Lt. Clifton-Jones became General Montgomery.

He was immediately driven to an airport and flown to Gibraltar where no attempt to conceal his new identity was made. From Gibraltar he was flown to Algiers where rumours of his impending arrival on an important mission had already been spread around. There he was extensively paraded, leading enemy agents to believe that an invasion of the south of France was imminent.

Meanwhile, D-Day, 6 June was approaching so a coded message was sent to the French Resistance Movement advising that plans for an Allied landing were ready to be put into action. Immediately bridges were blown up, telephone lines cut, railways demolished and roads strewn with mines. Aircraft destroyed enemy batteries while naval guns smashed concrete fortifications, and in spite of unfavourable weather, over 4000 ships transported huge Allied armies across the Channel, taking the enemy completely by surprise. Then began an all-out assault on German defences. The real Monty was in command, his double in Cairo.

By 26 June, Cherbourg had been captured, and high-ranking German officers suspecting they were now facing defeat, began plotting to assassinate Hitler who, however, had a secret weapon which was ready to be used. It was the V-1 (buzz bomb or doodlebug, so called), a pilotless plane with an explosive warhead. Again the target was London, bringing a new terror to the hapless citizens of the capital.

Although anti-aircraft guns in due course overcame the problem of the V-1s, relief was short-lived for an even deadlier weapon, the V-2, a rocket bomb, was sent across the Channel to target London yet again.

In Scotland we escaped these flying missiles and towards the end of June we staged a second show in Garrowhill school. Reports of its success resulted in our being invited to take the show up country to Broughton to give two evening performances in the village hall there, the proceeds to be given to the war effort. This meant that staff, pupils and parent helpers had to be accommodated in local houses for two nights.

We packed up our costumes and stage props and set off by bus shortly after lunch on the day of the first show. On arrival, my colleague, Anne, and I were driven by car to a lovely farmhouse where hospitality equalled that of *Woodside*, Aberfeldy. On the morning after the first performance, which was very well received, the farmer's wife brought us breakfast in bed, and of course you've guessed, the tray contained tea, toast and new-laid boiled eggs!

After breakfast we were taken by car to the centre of the village where members of the WVS had organised a Fair. It was a glorious day so it was an outdoor event and soon the tables that had been groaning under a mind-boggling display of home-made scones, pancakes, loaves, cream sponges, jams and chutneys, had been relieved of their entire burden ~ but not before Anne and I had managed to secure some home-baking to take back with us.

Next we visited a stall displaying knitted garments, embroidered tea and tray cloths, soft toys and a variety of knick-knacks. Among them I saw a pile of six lovely damask table napkins. They were unpriced so I asked an assistant what they cost. She had no idea and consulted the lady in charge of the stall. They seemed to be having some difficulty but eventually they came up with a price I was willing to pay and indeed for their quality I reckoned I had done rather well.

The second evening performance attracted so many spectators that before the show began it was 'standing room only' and as the programme progressed there was very little air circulating in the packed village hall and we all finished up completely exhausted. So, back at the farmhouse, after a refreshing cup of tea (and some home baking), Anne and I retired to our twin-bedded room and flaked out.

Before I had entered the real world in the morning there was a knock on the bedroom door. Was I, by any chance, the person who had bought six table napkins? They were not for sale! I felt as if I had stolen them but hastily took them downstairs to the waiting person who explained that they belonged to her mistress ~ the Lady of the Manor~ and they were part of a large set of napkins, initialled on one corner. They had been covering home baking and when that sold out she had taken them with her to the soft goods' stall and laid them there ready to be taken home. I handed them over with profuse apology. My money was refunded, but to my embarrassment, and in spite of my protests, the messenger insisted that she had been instructed that I should keep two of them. I have them still.

At the end of June I resigned from my temporary post in Garrowhill school for the very good reason that I was expecting a baby in October 1944, but when the baby (a girl) arrived it was some considerable time before her father was granted leave to see her. When at last he was, regretfully his daughter would have nothing to do with the 'stranger' who had suddenly appeared in the household.

Two's Company!

CHAPTER 26

Prophetic Vision

By January 1945 the Nazis were in full retreat. Paris had been liberated and British and American troops were advancing into Germany from the west while Russian troops were nearing Berlin on the east.

Hitler reputedly committed suicide in his bunker and his successor, Doenitz, surrendered unconditionally. On 8 May, VE Day, the war in Europe was declared to be ended. The war with Japan, however, had still to be concluded but the timescale was a short one. On 6 August the Americans dropped an atomic bomb on the Japanese city of Hiroshima, wiping it out and killing hundreds and hundreds of people. On 8 August Russia declared war on Japan, and on the same day the Americans dropped a second atomic bomb, this time on the Japanese city of Nagasaki, inflicting horrific damage and loss of life. On 14 August a Japanese unconditional surrender was announced. World War Two was over at last!

I remember little of VJ Day other than the fact that we had no outward celebration, respecting the grief of our neighbours whose only son would not be among those demobbed in due course.

Within my own family circle, my husband, and indeed all my relations who had served in the forces, eventually returned, at least physically unharmed, from various parts of the world. Demob, of course, did not happen immediately. Apart from the immense organisation required for the demobilisation of service personel, women were now doing work previously done by men, and factories making munitions, planes and other war-related materials were having to change to the production of peace-time needs.

On 27 June 1945, Ian had his final posting, from Shetland to Cornwall, and he was demobbed in time for Christmas.

RAF War Service Medal

Now, sixty years on from the outbreak of *The Second World War*, Camlachie school buildings have been demolished. Modern housing occupies the site and surrounding streets. There is private housing on the site of Vinegar Hill and tramcars no longer rattle past. Beardmore's, a munitions factory during the war, has been replaced by an extensive modern shopping mall, aptly named *The Forge*, and with parking for hundreds of cars.

Aberfeldy still retains an unspoiled natural beauty. The names above many of the shops have changed as have the commodities within them. The old Breadalbane Academy building, although still in use has, in addition, a splendid new school and within the grounds a community leisure centre with swimming pool. Tourists explore *The Birks*, at the entrance to which there is a fitting memorial to local people killed in the First and Second World Wars.

Lest We Forget

The exterior of Garrowhill School looks much as it did during the war years except that additional classrooms have been erected in the playground to accommodate children from houses built after the war. The school roll today stands at 543, with no class exceeding 33 pupils.

Within the school there have been vast changes. The hall has been extended so that all pupils may come together in assemblies. This has been done by removing the stage and incorporating the 'changing room' behind it. Pupils sit in groups and are comfortably dressed in sweat shirts. The walls of corridors and classrooms, bereft during the war of pupils' writing and art work because of the acute shortage of paper, are today alive with colourful displays and writing, reflecting the variety of on-going events and educational experiences that provide contexts for expression in a variety of forms.

We, in Britain, are part of the European Community, linked directly to the Continent by the Channel Tunnel. Towns and villages here are twinned with towns and villages in Europe, and schools have joint projects with their European counterparts, so fostering an understanding of the history and culture of their respective countries. Garrowhill School, for instance, has forged links with schools in Italy, Austria and Finland with the following three-year development plan started in 1997 and based on the teachings of the Czech educationist, Comenius, and his belief in partnership.

Year 1   Making Friends with Europe
Year 2   Water – for life, devastation and pleasure, fantasy (artistic representation)
Year 3   History and Culture

The under-noted study visits have taken place:

February 1997 – Sicily: October 1997 – Glasgow: September 1998 – Joensuu

Exchange Visit – 11 Sicilian pupils and 3 adults for whom Garrowhill parents provided hospitality.

Garrowhill School with head teacher and some of the pupils.

The following extract from *The High Road of the Future* written by Winston Churchill in 1947 represents his vision of the future.

Should there not be a place for a pillar called Europe, the Mother Continent and fountain source not only of the woes but also of most of the glories of modern civilisation?

Let me now set forth what it is we have to do. All the people living in Europe must learn to call themselves Europeans, and act as such so far as they have political power, influence or freedom. Once the conception of being European becomes dominant among those concerned, a whole series of practical steps will be open.

First there must be a Council of Europe. It must seek the most free and fertile trade between all its members and must work for the abolition or at least the diminution of tariff barriers between member states. It must strive for economic harmony as a stepping-stone to economic unity. Next, the Council of Europe must reach out towards some common form of defence which will preserve order among, and give mutual security to its members and enable Europe to take an effective part in the decisions of the United Nations Organisation.

Inseparably woven with this is the approach to a uniform currency. Luckily coins have two sides so that one side can bear the national and the other the European superscription. Postage stamps, passports, trading facilities, European social reunions for cultural, fraternal and philanthropic objects will flow out naturally along the main channel.

If at the beginning the governments of the various countries are not able to take official action, strong organisations of a popular character must be formed. There is no reason to suppose that existing governments, although they may not immediately feel able to take the initiative, will be adverse. Mr Attlee, the British Prime Minister has declared, "Europe must federate or perish."

It may well be that everybody cannot join at once. The beginning must be made. The nucleus must be formed so that others can join as soon as they feel inclined or able. The ideal is so commanding that it can afford a gradual realisation. If, in this interval we can revive the life and unity of Europe and build high and commanding a world structure of peace which no one dare challenge, the most awful crisis of history will have passed away and the highroad of the future will again become open.

Many of Sir Winston Churchill's visions have been realised. Some, as yet, remain unresolved, but is not the war of words infinitely better than the war of bombs?